Jonathan T. Scott

The Concise Handbook of Management
A Practitioner's Approach

The Concise Handbook
of Management
A Practitioner's Approach

BEST BUSINESS BOOKS®
Robert E. Stevens, PhD
David L. Loudon, PhD
Editors in Chief

Doing Business in Mexico: A Practical Guide by Gus Gordon and Thurmon Williams

Employee Assistance Programs in Managed Care by Norman Winegar

Marketing Your Business: A Guide to Developing a Strategic Marketing Plan by Ronald A. Nykiel

Customer Advisory Boards: A Strategic Tool for Customer Relationship Building by Tony Carter

Fundamentals of Business Marketing Research by David A. Reid and Richard E. Plank

Marketing Management: Text and Cases by David L. Loudon, Robert E. Stevens, and Bruce Wrenn

Selling in the New World of Business by Bob Kimball and Jerold "Buck" Hall

Many Thin Companies: The Change in Customer Dealings and Managers Since September 11, 2001 by Tony Carter

The Book on Management by Bob Kimball

Concise Encyclopedia of Advertising by Kenneth E. Clow and Donald Baack

Application Service Providers in Business by Luisa Focacci, Robert J. Mockler, and Marc Gartenfeld

The Concise Handbook of Management: A Practitioner's Approach by Jonathan T. Scott

The Marketing Research Guide, Second Edition by Robert E. Stevens, Bruce Wrenn, Philip K. Sherwood, and Morris E. Ruddick

Marketing Planning Guide, Third Edition by Robert E. Stevens, David L. Loudon, Bruce Wrenn, and Phylis Mansfield

Concise Encyclopedia of Church and Religious Organization Marketing by Robert E. Stevens, David L. Loudon, Bruce Wrenn, and Henry Cole

The Economics of Competition: The Race to Monopoly by George G. Djolov

Market Opportunity Analysis: Text and Cases by Robert E. Stevens, Philip K. Sherwood, J. Paul Dunn, and David L. Loudon

Concise Encyclopedia of Real Estate Business Terms by Bill Roark and Ryan Roark

Concise Encyclopedia of Investing by Darren W. Oglesby

Marketing Research: Text and Cases, Second Edition by Bruce Wrenn, Robert E. Stevens, and David L. Loudon

The Concise Handbook
of Management
A Practitioner's Approach

Jonathan T. Scott

Best Business Books®
The Haworth Reference Press™
Imprints of The Haworth Press, Inc.
New York • London • Oxford

For more information on this book or to order, visit
http://www.haworthpress.com/store/product.asp?sku=5399

or call 1-800-HAWORTH (800-429-6784) in the United States and Canada
or (607) 722-5857 outside the United States and Canada

or contact orders@HaworthPress.com

Published by

Best Business Books® and The Haworth Reference Press™, imprints of The Haworth Press, Inc.,
10 Alice Street, Binghamton, NY 13904-1580.

Cover design by Jennifer M. Gaska.

Library of Congress Cataloging-in-Publication Data

Scott, Jonathan (Jonathan T.)
    The concise handbook of management : a practitioner's approach / Jonathan T. Scott.
       p. cm.
    Includes bibliographical references and index.
    ISBN-13: 978-0-7890-2647-7 (hc. : alk. paper)
    ISBN-10: 0-7890-2647-3 (hc. : alk. paper)
    ISBN-13: 978-0-7890-2648-4 (pbk. : alk. paper)
    ISBN-10: 0-7890-2648-1 (pbk. : alk. paper)
    1. Management—Handbooks, manuals, etc. 2. Industrial management—Handbooks, manuals,
etc. 3. Business—Handbooks, manuals, etc. I. Title.

HD38.15.S27 2004
658—dc22

                                          2005001190

To George G. Scott Jr.,
a successful executive, manager, and turn-around specialist
in the highly competitive American wire rope and cable industry
(and a great dad too!)

ABOUT THE AUTHOR

Born in Trenton, New Jersey, **Jonathan T. Scott** grew up in nine different states before attending Brevard College (Brevard, North Carolina) and graduating from Florida State University (Tallahassee, Florida) in 1987. He has since earned a language certification from the Universite de Bourgogne (Dijon, France), an MBA from Western International University (at its former London, UK, campus), and a teaching certificate from Oxford Brookes University (Oxford, UK).

Scott worked in the leisure and recreation industry for over twenty years before becoming a teacher. As a manager he earned his stripes, and a reputation, for turning around three separate businesses under difficult circumstances (the first occurred in a war zone). Currently on his third passport, he has lived and worked in eight different countries. He now lectures on business and management issues in Europe.

Apart from his numerous internationally published management articles, Scott's books include *Fundamentals of Leisure Business Success,* the highly acclaimed novels *Expedition* and *Days Captive,* and the upcoming *On Wings*—the story behind the most successful fighting unit in all of human history.

If you are interested in having Jonathan Scott speak with your employees or students about work and management issues, or simply wish to share your comments about this book, please feel free to send him a message via the following address:

Jonathan_T_Scott@hotmail.com

I slept and dreamt
that life was joy.
I woke and saw
that life was duty.
I acted, and behold!
Duty was joy.

Rabindranath Tagore
Calcutta, India

CONTENTS

PART II:
BASIC THOUGHTS ON AND THEORIES OF MANAGEMENT

PART IV:
THE BASICS OF BUSINESS

Preface

Why Another Book About Management?

My induction into teaching was a sink-or-swim affair. While investigating a business opportunity in Warsaw, Poland, I learned that a former corporate executive had "pulled a runner" at the country's most prestigious private business school (unable to cope with the responsibilities of teaching, she'd simply disappeared). Although I'd never taught anything before, someone asked if I'd be interested in replacing her. Simply put, no one else could be found at such short notice. I said yes even though it was three weeks into the semester and neither syllabus nor lecture notes could be found. Because I didn't know quite how to approach the job, I took a few minutes during the first class and asked the students to explain their expectations.

"Well, so far we sat through two boring lectures based upon nothing more than theory and definitions," one student said. He cast his eyes to the ground as if he'd blurted out something wrong.

"Do you know anything about management?" asked another.

"When is someone going to teach us something we can actually use?" muttered a third.

The rest of the class, an intriguing mixture of young men and women from half a dozen different countries, nodded their heads in agreement.

My head reared back. After more than twenty years of working as a business practitioner I couldn't believe my ears. These students were displaying the typical signs of customer disgruntlement. It was apparent that most of these students were eager to learn, desperate even, but after suffering from a stream of lecturers who seemed to put teaching at the bottom of their priority list, they were losing interest.

"The problem with universities today," stated a friend (an Ivy League University lecturer) to me in an e-mail later that week, "is that they're full of professional researchers who are amateur teachers."

From that moment on I decided to revert to basic business sense. I would listen to my customers' (the students') wants and needs and *act upon them.* Every theory or academic point I introduced in class would be accompanied by an interesting highlight or example of practical application that brought the point home. The way I figured it, the onus was upon me to have my students *want* to come to class and do well. Thankfully, as a part-time lecturer, I had no publishing pressures placed upon me. My emphasis could therefore be placed on preparing students to be good managers—not in having them memorize abstract theories or in using them as cheap labor to gather research data. Now all I needed was a good management book.

Teachers (including myself) notoriously turn into prima donnas when it comes to selecting course texts and now I know why. As I looked through the piles of available material, I could see only the faults. Most textbooks were incredibly verbose and full of hyperbole and/or questionable profiles (remember when **celebrity CEOs** such as Jeff Skilling, Bernie Ebbers, and Dennis Kozlowski were heralded, and when Enron, WorldCom, and Arthur Andersen were considered excellent companies?). Others had graphs and models that were either so oversimplified they were meaningless or needed the explanation of entire chapters to comprehend. Many more books were dead boring or contained Disneyesque-styled writing and explanations. Too many of them placed far too much emphasis on big corporations when more than 90 percent of the world's working people are employed by small to midsized businesses (I suspect it is big corporations that are doling out research grants so they get studied more). In addition, the voices behind these books were not bold enough. In other words, the people who wrote them didn't appear to have much management experience. But what really irked me was how most of these books gave little or no attention to the importance of customers. Everything, and I mean *everything,* a manager does must be customer oriented. Yet it's difficult to come to that conclusion when reading most management books. The word *customer* is barely mentioned. Undaunted, I continued searching. One book seemed to suggest that children's stories could solve business problems (it was actually a pretty good book, but a management course can't be based on children's stories). Others appeared to be designed as an author-publishing vehicle or as a means of self-promotion. A few did nothing but disparage opposing thinkers. Still more were based on a catchy title and/or a marketing gimmick. The majority were ridiculously over-priced. At one point I considered photocopying relevant academic papers and passing them out to students, but so many of these papers are written in such an unnecessarily complex manner that I soon thought better of burdening students with them.

My mind went back to the MBA program I attended in London, England, at Western International University. On the first day of a class titled "Finance and the Corporation," the instructor limped into the room (he was awaiting hip replacement surgery) and blinked at us through spectacles the thickness of Coke-bottle bottoms. We, the assembled students, were reduced to a hush. This man was rumored to be a part of almost every piece of accounting legislation passed in the United Kingdom and he was very intimidating.

"Over the past several decades, I've worked in over a dozen companies, not to mention five different countries," he stated in his introduction. "And every few months it seems some bright spark publishes a new theory about determining costs in a business. Indeed there are too many of these formulas out there now, each one more complex than the last. Yet despite this proliferation, only two are ever really used outside academia. And by the end of this term, those two—and only those two—are what you're going to know inside and out."

I decided to apply this type of thinking to my new teaching position. I concluded to keep it simple and give the students bits and pieces from my first book, *Fundamentals of Leisure Business Success* (The Haworth Press), combined with what readable and applicable material I could find from around the world. After two years of this process I'd gathered enough fundamental material to write a book on management in much the same way my finance professor had approached his subject: by sticking to the basics. And so, *The Concise Handbook of Management* was born. Is it biased? Yes. Is it scientific? No. Is anything new being presented? Not really. The vast majority of information contained in this book is, similar to most management books, a rehash of everything else that's out there. The difference is that this book approaches the subject from a practitioner's viewpoint. In other words, it discusses management with customers in mind. I didn't write this book to pitch a new management theory but to present the practical necessities of management from a manager's perspective.

Please note that nothing in these pages is designed to be prescriptive or omnipotent. Rather, *The Concise Handbook of Management* is meant to

- be motivating—to whet the appetite of readers and get them interested in probing further into the subject of management (which really is fascinating);
- be supplemental to and balanced against other management books (because what's presented here is certainly not definitive or all-encompassing);
- approach management in a way that is understandable, practical, and, yes, somewhat entertaining;
- not overload the reader (management is *not* a complicated subject); and
- be affordable.

To accomplish these objectives, this book has been laid out in short, condensed chapters that include many true stories and renowned case studies designed to assist in highlighting each section's main points. Important terms have been highlighted in bold print and included in the glossary. Topics are approached with the attitude that you, the reader, have enough intelligence and ability to determine if or how the issues raised can be applied to current or future work challenges. In the end, I suppose proof of the book's success will be measured by the sales figures. I hope you find the information presented here to be useful.

Acknowledgments

Many thanks are owed to those at The Haworth Press, whose efforts helped make this a better book. These people include Donna Biesecker, Tara Davis, Peg Marr, Jillian Mason-Possemato, Julie Bednar, Lindsey Lewis, and Dawn Krisko.

PART I:
BUILDING THE MANAGEMENT FOUNDATION

Chapter 1

What Is Management?

1: the act or art of managing: the conducting or supervising of something (as a business) **2:** judicious use of means to accomplish an end **3:** the collective body of those who manage or direct an enterprise

Merriam-Webster's Collegiate Dictionary

1: the control and organizing of a business or other organization **2:** ... also refers to the people who do this **3:** the way you control someone or something

Collins Cobuild English Language Dictionary

1: the art or practice of managing (especially a business or money) **2:** the people in charge of a company or industry **3:** skill in dealing with people or situations (judgment)

Longman Dictionary of Contemporary English

1: the application of skill or care in the manipulation, use, treatment, or control of things or persons, or in the conduct of enterprise, operation or organization of commercial enterprise

The New Oxford English Dictionary

1: planning, organizing, leading and controlling the use of resources to accomplish goals

A popular definition seen in many textbooks

1: overseeing the work of others

A classic definition

By any stretch of the imagination, there will probably never be a shortage of management definitions or management job titles (see Exhibit 1.1). The problem with most definitions of management is that they only tell part of the story. For example, in the definitions previously mentioned (indeed in every definition of management I've ever seen) the word *customer* isn't seen. This is astonishing because servicing customers is the crux of *every* business organization. Equally as remiss is that most writers neatly filter out human nature in their descriptions of management. Let's face it, aseptic words and terms are great for dictionaries and academic tomes but they're terrible when it comes to explaining, warts and all, the full scope of what management entails. So how can the art and science of management be summed up in a few succinct words? Well, truth be told, it can't. Management is about more than leading, controlling, planning, organizing, and setting goals and objectives. Much more.

EXHIBIT 1.1. Three Basic Categories of Management Positions

TOP MANAGERS (ADMINISTRATORS)

Presidents
Managing directors
Vice presidents
CEOs (chief executive officers)

MID-LEVEL MANAGERS

Department heads
District managers
Unit chiefs

FRONTLINE MANAGERS

Supervisors
Foremen
Coordinators
Team or project leaders

Perhaps the best way to present a richer and more accurate concept of management is to look at what good managers do—or are *supposed* to do—in the course of a typical working day. Good managers constantly streamline their organizations toward making a sale. In other words, good managers keep their organizations on track by ensuring that everything that's being done is geared toward providing what customers want. In this regard, a good manager is responsible for reducing ambiguity, keeping costs down, and motivating others to do the same. In the same vein, good managers regularly take educated risks and exercise good judgment. These risks include trying new approaches, successfully adjusting to constant change, developing subordinates (good managers aren't afraid of letting other people shine—in fact they encourage it), and improving their own skills.

Since most managers are responsible for more work than one person can normally perform, a good manager delegates and integrates the work of others by acting as a clear channel of communication within the businesses they serve. Good management is about rising above the often monotonous grind of a working day and injecting motivation, creativity, discipline, and enthusiasm into areas in which they either don't exist or they're not wanted. It entails doing things you don't want to do in order to get and do the things you want. And while all this is occurring, the ups and downs of life in general must be successfully dealt with, such as fear, insecurity, births, deaths, romances, divorces, physical injuries, bad-hair days, bad-manner days, personal failings, and attitude problems to name a very few. Again, I'm talking about *good* managers. These are the men and women who face problems, put in long hours, set a good example, and have an inherent knack to create something from nothing. Good managers work well with others (including those they don't like) and can be counted on to be honest and upstanding. They concentrate on goals and results rather than showing who's boss, because the creed they live by is *integrity, responsibility,* and *maturity.* This means financial figures aren't manipulated and production numbers aren't fiddled with. That's not to say that good managers always score; they most certainly do not, but when good managers don't succeed the first time they pick themselves up, brush themselves off, learn from what happened (without blaming others), and *then* score. Good managers create value. In other words, they don't make excuses; they produce results.

Sound like a tall order? Well, it's not so high that it can't be reached. The truth is that there are tens of thousands of good managers in this world quietly going about their work and performing admirably. That most of them don't attract attention to themselves, in part, shows their management acumen and the dedication they have for their craft. Good managers understand that management isn't merely a rank; it's a responsibility, and they more often than not let their work speak for itself. They don't need to be charlatans, actors, or showpeople. Yes, a little bit of flashiness sometimes goes a long way in business; nevertheless, *prioritizing* showmanship is not the mark of a good manager.

Now let's look at the other side of the coin. What constitutes bad management? Simply put, bad managers are insecure, overbearing, dictating bosses who, in the long run, do little more than manage to get to work on time, instill fear in others instead of respect, barely put in an eight-hour day (or less) of real work, collect a paycheck, and/or maintain the status quo when opportunities abound. At an administrative level, bad managers tend to see their profession as only a game of acquisitions and mergers or act as though what they do involves only numbers.

Calling yourself a manager doesn't make you one in the same manner that cooking dinner doesn't make you a chef, penning a letter doesn't make you a writer, and going jogging doesn't make you an athlete. For those of you who think management is glamorous, well, placing the word *manager* on your door or a business card isn't an invitation to a gold-encrusted club and a bottomless expense account. Most management positions, particularly those in small to midsized businesses, aren't glamorous and don't come with perks. A business's resources are best spent serving *customers*—not managers— and that involves deflating one's ego,* rolling up one's sleeves, and working with everyone in an organization's hierarchical structure. In this regard, management is not about you. It's about serving others.

I often tell anyone who'll listen that although managing a business isn't the easiest thing in the world to do, too many teachers and students try to make it as complex as brain surgery. Certainly management, like so many other tasks, can be made as complicated as you'd

---

*Winston Churchill was once asked if he was flattered by the size of the crowds that came to hear him speak. "Yes," he replied, "but then I remind myself that if I was being hanged the crowds would be twice as big."

like, but the truth of the matter is that it needn't be complex. Nor is it dry and boring. In most cases management is fascinating—or at least it should be. (It's based on the study of human nature for heaven's sake. Who among us isn't intrigued by money, influence, passion, achievement, success, failure, greed, good deeds, and similar emotions, attributes, and weaknesses?) What else besides management demands the successful maneuvering of the strengths and weaknesses of those who perform it alongside those being managed? What else besides romance, sport, and warfare constantly tries and tests an individual both personally and against others?

Suffice it to say that all these factors combined with planning, organizing, leading, and controlling is a tough, relentless, and time-consuming job that demands regular assessment, constant improvement, and the ability to give more than is taken. And that, in part, is what makes management so difficult to define—let alone do.

Chapter 2

A Brief History of Management

Because before taking any journey, it's important to know where you've been, where you are, and which direction you're going.

Every day new technologies and innovations make our world a better place. Advancements on almost every front are being made at an astonishing rate. Yet when it comes to management, there isn't much that's new under the sun. If you traveled back in time thousands of years you'd probably be surprised to discover that we're really no more intelligent than our ancestors (i.e., our tools have changed, but human behavior hasn't). We live in a rather arrogant age in which too many people believe we have nothing to learn from the past. For a species that constantly relives its mistakes, this is a disturbing trend. Long before skyscrapers, multithousand-employee corporations, and the computer, people, not unlike us, built the great pyramids, the Great Wall of China, sailed the seas, explored the earth, and traded with far away lands. It took highly intelligent brains to do that.

Consider the pyramids, designed and built approximately 5,000 years ago by *people*—not a super human race of beings, not individuals anointed by Gods, and certainly not by alien intervention, but people—regular people who sat down, thought through, and carried out the entire process. Experts today concede that this monumental achievement, still unsurpassed today, was primarily the result of a well-managed, orderly system of volunteerism and rotating conscription. As proof of this, the ruins of medical facilities, housing areas, recreation grounds, kitchens, communal eating locations, and other remnants of a vibrant community project are scattered over the vast area surrounding the pyramids' bases. The general belief today is that it took 10,000 people twenty years to build the great pyramid—or perhaps 20,000 people ten years. Other sources state it took many more people and much more time. Either way, it took scores of competent managers to organize the stone cutters, labor crews, artists, and planners, as well as those who fed thousands of people every day, provided medical assistance, ran the housing areas, and so on. Force and fear alone cannot be attributed to the successful completion of such a massive project. Good management techniques had to be preeminent.

The same applies to the Great Wall of China, built thousands of years ago and still one of the only reported man-made objects (apart from light) observable on earth from space.

And what about the Romans? In their day the Romans conquered and governed most of Europe and parts of the Middle East and North Africa. After the Romans had conquered an area, the locals more often than not assimilated to the "enemy" way of life because the Roman lifestyle was much more advanced, better managed, and more comfortable than theirs.

The great cathedrals and artworks of Europe make for additional managerial examples. Take Michelangelo for example. It's been reported that when he died his house was virtually empty except for a bed alongside which stood a locked iron strongbox filled with today's equivalent of $8 million in gold coins. Did he acquire this breathtaking fortune from single-handedly sculpting and painting portraits? No. Michelangelo was an accomplished manager. When a work was commissioned (such as the Sistine Chapel, the Medici Chapel, or the Laurentian Library), he hired dozens, sometimes hundreds, of skilled workers, trained them to do exactly what he wanted, and kept meticulous employee timesheets and payment records. In fact, when he wasn't involved in his own personal artistry, much of Michelangelo's day was spent visiting and supervising his various project sites.

Then, after all of these accomplishments, in the course of numerous cycles of war, disease, religious intolerance, corruption, apathy, and famine, the managerial skills used to create the pyramids, the Greek temples, Rome, and most of the European masterpieces seemingly vanished—only to be reinvented by future generations in much the same way that concrete, formerly introduced by the Romans, had to be reinvented when it was needed again.

THE INDUSTRIAL REVOLUTION
AND THE DIVISION OF LABOR

In 1776, economist Adam Smith, in his famed treatise, *The Wealth of Nations,* advocated that dividing labor into manageable stages would greatly improve a business's production. No doubt some former civilization had previously reaped the benefits of this simple idea, but Smith had the good sense to write it down and publish it. His proposal centered on the idea that ironworkers made approximately 10 to 200 pins per day when they worked individually. However, he argued, if these workers were split into separate units with each unit responsible for a specific task, around 48,000 pins could be produced (e.g., one man would keep the fire stoked, another would operate the molds, and a third would extract the cooled wire and pass it onto others who cut, shaped, and sharpened the wire into pins).

So began the industrial revolution.

Some one hundred years later, Samuel Colt reinvented division of labor processes to mass produce firearms. Fifty years after Colt, Henry Ford reinvented the division of labor process by applying it to the building of automobiles.

THE STUDY OF MANAGEMENT BEGINS

From 1776 onward, the study of management continued in fits and starts right up to the twentieth century, specifically, 1911, when industry really took off. At that time a man named Frederick Taylor published a book titled *The Principles of Scientific Management.*

Taylor was by most accounts a rigid, prickly, and highly religious man (he was both a Quaker and puritan) who firmly believed that most workers were inherently lazy. Unable to bide this, he made it his mission to rectify the situation. It should be noted that in this period of history, Taylor had a point. Workers tended to take as long as possible to complete a job and management usually consisted of on-the-spot decisions made by an untrained foreman. Little or no emphasis was made to match worker skills with the job at hand and any sense of personal responsibility was virtually nonexistent. Apart from trained craftsmen, unskilled workers had a reputation for caring little about their work.

In response, in 1901, at the Midvale Steel Company in Pennsylvania, using workers loading iron ore (in units that weighed ninety-two pounds each) into boxcars as his core project, Taylor began experimenting with his theories. On one day he had a worker (a man named Schmidt) use one type of tool to load the boxcars. On another day a different tool would be used. The following day, Taylor would tell Schmidt to walk while bending his knees. The next, he would be asked to keep his legs straight. On and on it went.

In the meantime, Taylor calculated the number of minutes it took Schmidt to perform each task as well as the total amount of iron ore he could load onto the trains. After much experimentation, Taylor concluded that there was one most effective method of loading boxcars. As he predicted, taking the time to figure this out resulted in a 400 percent increase in productivity! Word spread. By 1908 Harvard University declared Taylor's methods of scientific management to be the basis upon which all its business courses would be set. However, the ball didn't really start rolling until 1910. In that year the United States convened a court trial to determine why the country's railroad owners wanted to raise transport rates. During the subsequent hearings, a disciple of Taylor took the stand and testified that the railroads didn't need to raise their rates. Instead, if they employed scientific methods of management, they could save $1 million a day. This was an inconceivable amount of money at the turn of the twentieth century, and the gasp of astonishment that arose in the courtroom spread like wildfire across the United States, as well as overseas. The age of efficiency had begun.

THE EVOLUTION OF SCIENTIFIC MANAGEMENT

In the decades that followed, Taylor's work was examined, used, and enhanced by many others. Included in this frenzy is the work of Frank and Lillian Gilbreth. Early in their careers the Gilbreths attended one of Taylor's lectures and decided to join the cause. They were among the first to use motion pictures to study and improve human movement in the workplace, and they became famous for reducing the amount of motions necessary for laying bricks from eighteen to five, thereby tripling productivity. They also championed the development of specialized tools to improve worker performance.

Through their work the notion of scientific management continued to spread.

At about the same time, management studies began spiraling off into different areas. Whereas Frederick Taylor concentrated on mid- to bottom-level management, others began looking at top-level administration and management as a whole. Equally as important, the classification of management split into separate directions. For the sake of discussion, these two approaches can be considered the *administrative approach* (which views management as something akin to a caste system that focuses on tasks) and the *humanistic approach* (which envisions management as a means of motivating others to increase productivity).

The administrative approach had in its corner an academic named Max Weber (pronounced *vay-ber*). Writing in the early 1900s, Weber's idea of management involved a strict hierarchy of authority that he named **bureaucracy.** It's important to remember here that Weber conceived his theory in a different time and age than exists today. In part, bureaucracy was created as a means of eschewing nepotism and favoritism. Then, as now, these unfair practices denied too many people a place in the employment loop. Weber also realized that his ideas would probably never work in the real world—something few academics ever admit. Instead, his intention was for managers to focus on the positive aspects of bureaucracy (rationality, technical competence, authoritarianism, and impersonality) via the following practices:

- Jobs should be broken down into simple, routine, and well-defined tasks (division of labor).
- Offices and positions should be arranged in a hierarchical order.
- All managers and workers should be selected on the basis of their qualifications.
- Formal rules and regulations should be used to ensure uniformity and discipline.
- Rules and controls should be impersonal and applied uniformly.
- Managers should be hired from within.

Around this same period a man named Henri Fayol took a different approach. Unlike Weber, Fayol was an actual practitioner (he was the managing director of a coal mining firm) who developed a list of points designed to improve an organization's efficiency. He called them the fourteen universal truths or principles of management. They are as follows:

- Work should be divided into specializations (division of labor).
- Managers must have the authority to make **rules** and give orders.
- Employees must obey and respect these orders.
- Each employee should receive orders from only one superior.
- Each set of activities should be directed by one manager with one plan.
- The interests of one employee or employee group cannot take precedence over an **organization.**
- Workers must be paid a fair wage for the jobs they perform.
- A business must determine beforehand if employees can do a job on their own or if a managerial hierarchy is needed.
- Communication should follow a **chain of command.**
- People and materials should be in the correct place at the correct time (i.e., **planning** is essential).
- Managers should be kind and fair to their employees.
- A high rate of employee turnover is inefficient and should be avoided.
- Employees who are allowed to actively participate in the design and implementation of their work will work harder.
- Promoting team spirit will build harmony and unity within a business. (Fayol, 1916)

Today, many of these points seem so patently obvious that, again, it must be remembered that both Weber and Fayol were making bold statements for their time. Simply put, the industrializing world was ripe with the stench of inhumane practices—child labor and twelve-hour workdays being only two. Most employees lived and worked in appalling conditions and both Weber and Fayol, in their own distinct way, wanted to introduce improvements that benefited worker, manager, and business owner alike.

Other Movers and Shakers of Note

If Frederick Taylor can be called the "father of management," then Mary Parker Follet is almost certainly its mother. At the time of

World War I, when most workers were considered little more than uneducated servants, Follet, working out of Boston, preached the unpopular idea that employees were valuable assets who had the ability to add greatly to their work if their ideas and complaints were listened to. Her conclusion was that managers and workers should operate as a team. The result, she said, would be an increase in workplace harmony and productivity. At a time when most people thought workers should neither be seen nor heard, her thoughts were not welcomed with open arms.

Hugo Munsterberg is another management scientist worth mentioning. As early as 1913, Munsterberg recommended that businesses should adopt psychological testing as a means of selecting the best employee for a job. He also used testing to determine the best training methods and motivation techniques for use with employees. Nearly one hundred years later, many of Munsterberg's ideas, or variants of them, are still in use today.

Last on this list, Chester Barnard, then president of the New Jersey Bell Telephone Company, advocated in 1938 that businesses were social environments that not only had responsibilities to their workers but also to customers, communities, suppliers, investors, and other stakeholders. Again, at a time when most people viewed a business as the personal property of an owner with which he or she could do whatever he or she wanted, this was not a popular notion. Despite Barnard's teachings, the human element is today still taken for granted in most businesses.

PERHAPS THE MOST IMPORTANT STUDY OF ALL

Between 1924 and 1932, the Western Electric Company, operating out of their Hawthorne Works factory in Chicago, Illinois, began a series of revolutionary experiments. Hawthorne Studies, as they came to be called, began with the desire to discover what made employees more productive (the Hawthorne plant assembled telephone equipment and similar electrical components). Researchers began their experiments by trying to ascertain whether a connection existed between environment and productivity.

The first observations began with an increase in factory lighting. Several tests were conducted in which the brightness of the room was intensified. The conclusion was that brightening the workroom did indeed cause an increase in productivity. Incredibly, worker absences decreased as well. However, when researchers later turned down the lights they discovered that the same thing happened! Furthermore, as the lights were turned down lower, productivity continued to increase until it became so dark no one could see.

In another experiment, a silent person did nothing but sit and take notes in a room full of workers. Again, researchers watched in amazement as productivity increased and worker absences decreased.

In a third experiment the workers were told that if productivity increased their wages would increase proportionately. In other words, the harder each person worked, the more he or she would be paid. Astonishingly, productivity levels decreased.

Years later, it was determined that what had made the workers in the first two experiments more productive (and more apt to come to work) wasn't due to the amount of lighting or the act of being observed. Instead, the workers had been made to feel important, more secure, and in some ways more accepted by their company by taking part in the experiments. These factors made them work harder. The third experiment took longer to analyze. In the end, interviews with the employees concluded that because they were being paid more to produce more, a feeling was generated that perhaps management was trying to weed out slower workers. As a result, the employees had banded together when not being observed in order to come up with their own idea of what constituted a proper work output. That way, everyone could meet an agreed-upon target and no one would be reprimanded or fired. Money, that recreant, age-old, cure-all proved to be less of a motivator than job security.

Those Who Don't Study History Are Doomed to Repeat It

In the early 1990s, an American company bought a boiler factory in Warsaw, Poland. Armed with technology and the latest managerial practices the company set out to make their new acquisition more productive and cost efficient. In the process, just as in the Hawthorne experiments, factory employees were told that the harder they worked the more they would be paid. This concept usually worked in the United States so it was bound to work in a country where the average monthly paycheck was less than what most Americans made in a week. Right? Wrong! Productivity in the factory took a downward turn until, months later, someone took the time to get to know the employees and ask them what it was they most wanted from their job. Job security was their reply.

To Be Continued . . .

Although the Hawthorne Studies were instrumental in shattering the notion that employees are nothing more than servants who should be devoid of emotion, feeling, and the need to be respected—and should therefore be treated as such—many academics still see the studies as unscientific, flawed, inconclusive, and just plain dumb. The truth is that they opened the door to understanding that every workplace is unique, every group of people is unique, and every manager has his or her work cut out for him or her in determining what works best for business improvement. They also helped prove the old maxim "management seeks efficiency; workers seek motivation."

And so it continues today as managers and management researchers continue to take sides, denounce others, and disregard history when insisting that business success results only from one of the two age-old managerial categories: administrative or humanistic.

Chapter 3

The First Three Steps
to Becoming a Good Manager

An ancient Chinese proverb suggests that a journey of a thousand miles begins with a single step. We're going to begin with three.

STEP 1: MIND-SET

Nothing occurs in a vacuum. In business, this means that above-average amounts of the following attributes are needed before anyone can become a good manager:

Ambition: an overwhelming desire to succeed

Commercial intellect: the ability to scan business environments for weaknesses, threats, and opportunities

Perseverance: being steadfast and consistent (not stubborn) with your goals no matter what happens

Resilience: the capacity to learn from mistakes, brush off adversity, and pull yourself together

The will to win: the commitment and dedication to make real sacrifices and come out on top rather than merely participate*

In other words, the first step toward becoming a good manager is to have a good attitude. How is a good attitude acquired? Much the way most achievements are accomplished: through practice and refinement. To be a good manager you have to want to successfully control

---

*The will to win is aptly depicted in modern-day, big-city marathons. Although thousands of people participate in these marathons, realistically only a dozen or so can expect to win. The others are happy to just finish the course. As a manager, it's not enough to finish the course. Each and every day a good manager must set out to win.

your life and its direction. It also helps to know and care about the industry you've chosen to enter. You should learn about its history as well as the heroes, villains, and everyday people who comprise it. You need to formulate an idea for where you and the industry want to go and establish a concept for the role you want to play. A successful attitude, if it's to grow at all, will come from these interests.

Many years ago I attended a seminar presented by a man widely regarded as one of the world's foremost authorities on throwing the javelin. Potbellied, chain-smoking, and possessing an astonishingly colorful vocabulary, this man looked as different from an athlete as anyone could possibly be. Indeed, during the question-and-answer session that followed, an attendee asked him point-blank how he had become such an expert.

"Well, I certainly didn't set out to be," he replied, "In fact, I'm a house painter and have never attended college. But when my son announced that he was taking up the sport, I decided to look into it. At that time I didn't know anything about the javelin so I read a couple of books. That led to attending seminars and contacting experts in the field—all of whom were quite keen on sharing their passion. One step led to another and before I knew it I was hooked. Years later, the words 'leading authority' were used in conjunction with my name. I guess it all comes down to the fact that instead of sitting on the sidelines I got interested. That led to getting involved, and once I got involved I didn't want to stop."

STEP 2: INTEGRITY

Simply put, good managers are honest people; they don't lie to others and they don't lie to themselves. It's been said that for every corporate crook there are at least ten corporate deceivers: people who fool themselves into thinking that situations are different from what they appear to be. Deception or dishonesty—call it what you want—either way, it constitutes bad management. Remember the corporate scandals of 2002 and the around-the-clock media coverage of dozens of disgraced companies? In a perverted desire to excel, the managers running these businesses somehow made conscious decisions that the ends were more important than the means. Greed and unchecked ambition became their measure of success. Ironically, before these scandals broke, many respected media outlets repeatedly told viewers and readers that these companies as well as their managers should be admired and emulated. Unfortunately, the people managing these highlighted businesses turned out to be nothing more than charlatans. In every conceivable way they lacked the stoic integrity and quiet pragmatism that good managers radiate.

As a former business practitioner I'm completely baffled whenever I see managers throwing honesty by the wayside. In business, honesty isn't an option; it's an imperative. If you don't think this is true ask yourself the following question: If I have a choice between doing business with an honest person (or business) or a dishonest one, which will I choose? The following story illustrates this point.

I once led a firm that oversaw approximately two dozen business sites scattered across a large Middle-Eastern city. One of these sites consisted of a cavernous building hired out to organizations for corporate affairs, art exhibits, fashion shows, product displays, children's programs, theater groups, film showings, and so forth. One day I was approached by a group of men interested in setting up a three-day trade show to kick off a new product line. I greeted them and gave them directions to the building's booking office.

"Thank you," they replied. One of the men then extended his arm and a brand new, wide-screen color television was pushed into my office.

"As a token of our appreciation," he said.

For several seconds I gazed at the television in amazement. "That's not necessary," I finally stammered.

The men stared back.

"Really, it's not necessary," I insisted. "If you want to book the exhibition hall all you need to do is put down a deposit."

The men glanced at each other, shrugged their shoulders, and left with the television.

Confused by this, I told my employees what had happened at the next staff meeting.

"You mean you didn't take the television?" they asked incredulously.

"Of course not," I replied.

They laughed. Apparently, my predecessors had all demanded gifts *in addition to a rental fee* as their regular way of conducting business. It suddenly became apparent why exhibition hall bookings were so difficult to procure. A few weeks later, a Persian rug seller also tried to give me a gift before renting out the hall, which I turned down as well. Two months passed before I was next approached, but this time it was under vastly different circumstances.

"Your cashier has informed us that there is a three-month waiting period for booking your exhibition hall," a visiting sales team said. "Unfortunately, we can't wait that long."

"Three months? That's impossible," I replied. I asked them to follow me to the office.

"What's going on?" I whispered to the cashier. "We can't afford to turn business away. For crying out loud, if these people want to book the building, do it."

"But sir," the cashier replied, "the building *is* fully booked for the next three months."

Stunned, I reached across her desk to check the calendar. Indeed, every available time slot was taken for the following twelve weeks. My head reeled with astonishment. "What's prompted this?" I mumbled.

"Word's gotten around that no one has to pay us a bribe anymore," she explained.

STEP 3: TRAINING

It's been said that the only situation in which one starts at the top is when digging a hole. In management, as with so many other career options, if one begins at the top with no experience that hole usually becomes the digger's grave. Training helps resolve problems of inadequacy and ignorance. Because the best indicator of future behavior is past behavior, and the road to good management is paved with past mistakes and failures, it is crucial to want to continuously learn and do better. The reason for doing so is not to draw up a plan so you can charge into the future, but to develop enough skills so that almost *any* plan can be put into action. One of the essentials in becoming a good manager is to be flexible and sustain the ability to rapidly take action. Only then can you handle almost anything the future may throw at you.

To put it differently, good managers, like good athletes, continuously hone their skills while carrying in their gut a desire to go for it. Good managers aren't interested in maintaining the status quo. They want to shake things up and seek out new opportunities—not in a sloppy, fanatical, all-out campaign that withers away after a few days or weeks—but rather in a series of actions that lead to small, achievable successes from which they and the people they manage can gather encouragement. Please note that this is not something that can happen overnight. It takes patience and much practice in

- dealing with others (motivating people and successfully playing politics);
- handling responsibility;
- wringing as much as possible out of a business's culture (working *within* an established system and knowing when and how to bend the rules without breaking the law, without being unethical, or without acting selfishly);
- establishing market share (ethically taking no prisoners) and looking ahead; and
- understanding, accepting, and *acting upon* the concept that a manager's duty is to serve others.

In essence, upon becoming a manager you learn that you've begun to have control over your work. Not all of it, but some of it. Through trial and error you learn that you *can* make a difference and that you *can* do things differently. Just as important, good managers must take into account the motivation and well-being of others—actions that don't come naturally in a world in which we're all fighting for our professional lives. A man that spent his life building a successful business once summed this up beautifully when asked how he had accomplished so much. "The way I look at it," he replied, "is that I didn't build this business. It built me."

I'll finish this chapter with an illustrative joke:

Two men run into each other thirty years after attending the same university. One is a college professor. The other is an extraordinarily wealthy businessman.

"How did you do it?" asked the professor. "Of all people, how in the world did you end up succeeding at business?"

"Well," replied the other man, "somewhere along the way I learned to buy things at one dollar and sell them for two dollars. And it's that one percent difference that's made me what I am today."

The point is that genius doesn't guarantee managerial success. More often than not it's attitude, integrity, and school-of-hard-knocks training that matters most.

Chapter 4

Understanding the Importance
of Customers

In the summer of 2001, I began a new job as the general manager of a $15 million water park nearing completion in the Far East. Within a week of arriving I knew much work lay ahead. For instance, although the children's swimming area was designed for 400 occupants, I was told that only two lifeguards would be employed. "Two lifeguards is a start," I suggested to the woman who, up to this point, had been overseeing the project, "but two people watching over four hundred children is difficult to do on dry land. If water is added to the equation, there's an even greater risk of—"

The woman spun around as if she'd been slapped. "Hiring more lifeguards is not in the plan," she snapped.

We continued our tour in silence. Looking around, I noticed that the park, designed to accommodate 6,000 people, contained only three small food kiosks set up in short-order-cook style. A fourth operation was envisioned as a luxurious restaurant complete with linen tablecloths and uniformed waiters. The small area it encompassed could serve only fifty customers at a time. In a bid to be diplomatic I pointed out the many good things that were being done in the park before mentioning the food service issue. "Most people eat lunch around noontime, and with thousands of people in attendance that'll put a huge demand on the food kiosks," I said. "Maybe if the kiosks are redesigned in a fast-food-restaurant style we can resolve any problems before they occur."

"But we don't want fast food here," the woman interjected. Her eyes narrowed. "The people on this island don't eat hamburgers and french fries."

"No, no," I said, "I'm talking about a fast-food *setup*. The kiosks can serve anything customers wish. It just needs to be served quickly."

"But that's not what we want," she retorted.

I carefully mentioned a few more positive things before continuing. "In water parks," I said, "almost everyone is wearing a bathing suit. So is a restaurant with linen tablecloths and uniformed waiters our best option? With only fifty customers serviceable at any one time, not to mention the children running around—"

"But this type of restaurant is what our chairman wants," she explained.

"Of course the wants and needs of the chairman are important," I replied, "but at the end of the day everything a business does must be designed with its customers in mind."

She stared at me for ten long seconds before uttering the most astonishing words I've ever heard in my professional life. "That's no way to run a business," she snorted. "In a proper business, everything must come from the top down."

Needless to say, I didn't last long at the job. By the end of the month the woman had me kicked off the island and soon another general manager took my place. He lasted six months. Some time later I received an e-mail from the recreation director of a resort close to where the waterpark had opened. "The park is a complete disaster," he stated, "so much so that we've decided not to send our guests there." Another e-mail, from the liaison company that had set up my initial interview for the job, was even more specific. "No one has been paid, many people are angry, and the government is opening an investigation. To top it off, 'Mrs. X' [the woman who'd showed me around] has disappeared."

Fifteen years before accepting the waterpark job I worked for a fitness club that decided to change its billing operation to a direct debit format. At the time, direct debit was a new concept and most customers were reluctant to sign over authorization giving a business the right to automatically deduct monthly fees from their bank accounts. The manager, however, was adamant. One day a man came in to buy a year's membership for his son. As I began to explain our direct debit policy, he pulled out a wad of cash. "I'd like to pay with this if you don't mind," he said.

At that moment the club's manager walked by. "What are you doing?" he asked.

"I'm signing this man's son up," I said.

"Is everybody around here deaf?" he bellowed. "Payments can be made only by direct debit."

Of course the customer left. And so did I two months later. Not long after that the business collapsed. But I guess the manager had shown everyone who was boss.

LOSING TOUCH

What is it that causes so many otherwise intelligent people to lose sight of the fact that to make money and survive a business must focus on its customers? Perhaps this rather astonishing oversight can be attributed to *sensory adaptation*. **Sensory adaptation** is the human body's inclination to eventually ignore the stimulus of clothes, smells, eyeglasses, wristwatches, contact lenses, and almost anything else we need, get used to, and forget is there—until it's gone.

UNDERSTANDING EXTERNAL AND INTERNAL CUSTOMERS

Getting Back to Basics

According to Oakland (1993), a **customer** is everyone that an organization serves. Read this definition carefully because it includes *everyone* we come into contact with at work—not just the people whose money we take in exchange for a product or service. For reasons of clarity these people can be labeled as

> **external customers:** those who buy a business's products and services, and
>
> **internal customers:** those who are either employed by, use, or rely on the work of others within an organization (including suppliers, contractors, shareholders, the community in which the business is located, and other stakeholders).

Management 101

Lesson 1

The reason why external customers are important is because the money they exchange for goods and services pays for everything in the business (the taxes, bills, rent, salaries, materials, insurance, pensions, medical plans, equipment, and so on).

Lesson 2

The reason why internal customers (employees) are important is because without them business will not take place. Equally, *how internal customers are treated has a direct bearing on the way external customers are treated.* In other words, the basic responsibility of every person in any business is to serve everyone else. Think of the individuals within an organization as links in a chain. Now form a picture of a chain in your mind. Which link is the least important?

Lip Service versus Customer Service

External and internal customers are essential to every business. It doesn't take fancy schemes or dramatic expenses to win them over. Usually all that's needed is the human element: acknowledgment, respect, a smile, a listening ear, politeness, and honesty. Gimmicks, slogans, or the latest trendy management theory rarely amount to much when attracting or retaining customers.

Not long ago I stood in line at a library waiting to check out a book. Behind the counter a group of employees earnestly attended to their duties. In the background a phone rang incessantly while one employee organized books on a trolley, a second typed on a computer, and a third searched for something in a drawer. So I stood there, along with four other customers, waiting for these people to finish whatever it was they were doing in order to get some service. One customer simply wanted to return a book (there were no convenient after-hour book drops). Another was trying to herd her kids together. Behind me an old man glanced at his watch. You would have thought we were invisible. The puzzling thing is that this was the most well-staffed library I'd ever seen. Employees were literally all over the place. And above them all hung a yellowing sign that read: THE CUSTOMER IS #1.

When budget cuts hit this library, the result was predictable. The knee-jerk reaction to money loss in so many businesses is to cut staff. Rarely does *improving service to attract more customers* come into play. Doing so involves too much hard work. Instead, employees and training are eliminated from the budget and customer platitudes are nailed to the wall. Some of the more popular include

> OUR CUSTOMERS ARE OUR FAMILY.
> WE ARE CUSTOMER DRIVEN.
> PEOPLE ARE OUR MOST IMPORTANT ASSET.
> THE CUSTOMER IS ALWAYS RIGHT.
> THE CUSTOMER IS KING.

The list is endless, yet, when you think of your own experiences as either an internal or external customer, how many times have you been subjected to rudeness, glued-on grins, unhappy repetitive responses, lies, or a generally uncaring or patronizing manner?

THE TEN COMMANDMENTS OF BUSINESS SUCCESS

One of the best examples in understanding the importance of customers was written by Graham Brooks, Managing Director of Dowman Car and Trucks in Stockport, England. His principles are difficult to contradict:

1. Customers are the most important people in our business.
2. Customers are not dependent on us; we are dependent on them.
3. Customers are not people with whom to argue or match wits.
4. Customers bring us their needs; it is our job to fill those needs.
5. Customers are not an interruption of work; they are the purpose of it.
6. Customers do us a favor when they call; we do not do them a favor by serving them.
7. Customers are part of our business; they are not outsiders.
8. Customers deserve the most courteous and attentive treatment we can give them.

9. Customers are the individuals who make it possible to pay our wages.
10. Customers are the lifeblood of this and every other business. (Scott, 1998)

Elementary Customer Mathematics (or Penny-Wise and Pound-Foolish)

Make no mistake, if customers are not happy with the service they're given they *will* take their business elsewhere. Studies show that a business can lose 20 percent of its external customers if its products are of poor quality, but 66 percent will be lost if the service itself is perceived as poor. Some estimates claim that it costs anywhere from five to ten times as much trying to attract new external customers than it costs to retain old ones. Also, keep in mind the costs of finding, hiring, and training internal customers (employees). I know many practitioners who quietly lament the fact that their companies spend a fortune finding and educating good people only to have them lured away by other businesses that appreciate them more. The message is clear: Winning over customers (both internal and external) is not only a necessity, it's an ongoing process requiring *regular* fine tuning and attention.

WHAT IS GOOD CUSTOMER SERVICE?

Profitable customer service begins with good ethics and includes truthful advertising, good phone etiquette, sincere attempts at quality, and *giving immediate attention*. In other words, it starts before the customer arrives at your business and continues long afterward. Everyone is ultimately responsible for creating a positive image. *No one is too busy to help.* No customer should be abandoned, or be made to feel abandoned, during or after they make contact with you. If you don't already know this then you need to memorize and practice it until it becomes second nature.

Dealing with Difficult Customers

Generally speaking, difficult customers are people whose cost of service outweighs what they generate in terms of revenue. Every business has them. Whether internal or external, there are several ways to treat difficult customers before taking the irrevocable step of showing them the door. When pride, the need to maintain dignity, or temper threaten to contaminate a customer relationship, a few proven tips may help diffuse the situation:

1. *Listen to the customer.* Don't just let the customer talk. *Listen.* The customer may have a valid point and is merely not presenting it appropriately. Don't interrupt and don't trivialize the problem. Instead, let the customer run out of steam.

2. *Remain calm.* Speak softly and directly. Lowering your voice almost always results in the person to whom you are speaking doing the same. Don't exacerbate the situation by becoming excited, matching wits, or trying to get the upper hand. Control the situation by controlling yourself. It's very difficult for difficult customers to play their "game" if the opposition refuses to play.

3. *Don't take any remarks or behavior personally.* Leave personal traits out of the situation. If you maintain your professionalism you will not lose dignity—no matter how much the other person is carrying on.

4. *Attempt to solve the problem.* Do not pass the buck by sending the customer away on a wild goose chase. The goal is to solve the problem quickly and directly. Remember that the customer may not know your organization's setup and may be frustrated because it's not obvious where to go for help.

5. *Apologize for any inconvenience and thank the customer.* Acknowledgement is a powerful tool for disarming aggression.

Something to Consider

If the importance of maintaining good, all-around customer service still hasn't sunk in, consider the story of Ray Kroc.

In the 1960s, Mr. Kroc was a salesman who sold milk-shake makers and other restaurant appliances. He became intrigued by a large order that a California customer made for milk-shake mixers and traveled across the country to find out why so many were needed. Ray thought that perhaps he could figure out why this customer needed more than the average number of mixers and use this reasoning to sell more mixers to other restaurants. The name of the restaurant he visited was called McDonald's (at the time a small chain of burger stands), and in no time at all Kroc became enamored of its simplified menu philosophy and the speed with which it served customers. As a result, he established such close relations (as a supplier) with the Mc-Donald brothers that he was the first person they approached when they decided to sell their business and retire. The rest is history. Kroc took the ball and ran with it and McDonald's became what it is today. The moral of the story? It was good customer service, both internal and external, that provided the means of forming what eventually became one of the most successful businesses in the world.

THE FINAL WORD

In an age in which acquisitions, mergers, and artificially inflating the price of stocks can take center stage (thereby taking management's eye off the ball), it's crucial to remember that creating a product or service and selling it to customers forms the essence of what business is about. Therefore, the purpose of the manager is to serve others (i.e., find customers and keep them). Put another way, fancy gimmicks, glitz, underhandedness, sleight-of-hand tricks, and fiddling with statistics are no match (or substitute) for shoe leather and elbow grease when it comes to running a business. Nothing in a business supersedes paying customers—and employees are the people who serve paying customers. Interpreting business any other way is a complete and utter waste of time and resources. Period.

PART II:
BASIC THOUGHTS ON AND THEORIES OF MANAGEMENT

Chapter 5

Management Competencies
and Styles

Despite evidence to the contrary, many businesses are under the impression that good managers come only from within one industry. In other words, good hotel managers must come from the hotel industry, good retail managers must be trained in the retail trade, and so on. Although promoting from within is a noble and sometimes appropriate policy, doing so blindly without considering the talents and freshness that an outsider brings to a managerial job can lock an organization into a cyclical course that merely repeats its bad habits. The leisure industry for example (hotels in particular), is rife with this practice, which in some cases amounts to little more than managerial incest. The truth is that good managers can be competent in a variety of fields if they concentrate on two overriding factors: (1) the ability to get the most from employees, and (2) the needs and wants of customers.

Many years ago, British Airways suffered from one of the worst reputations in the airline industry. For the most part this notoriety was attributed to poor service. Desperate to make improvements, the company's chairman decided a radical change was in order. Shock waves resulted as the former head of an American rental car agency was named as British Airways' new CEO.

"Ridiculous!" screamed the critics. "Ludicrous!"

But British Airways was soon on the mend and eventually found itself at or near the top of several "World's Best Airlines" lists (it has since run into other difficulties, but that's another story). Bear in mind that before this turnaround occurred most airline CEO's were either former pilots or had worked in the flight industry all of their lives. But British Airways' new CEO didn't have a pilot's license or indeed any aviation experience. Apparently, British Airways thought there were enough people in the company who could advise him on things of that nature. Instead, his strengths lay in being competent, which was just what the airline needed.

MANAGERIAL COMPETENCIES

Competencies in management can more or less be classified into the following two categories:

1. General management skills:
   - *Conceptual skills:* the ability to comprehend complex situations
   - *Interpersonal skills:* the ability to work with, understand, and motivate other people
   - *Political skills:* the ability to network as well as gain allies and gather power
   - *Technical skills:* the ability to understand and apply specialized knowledge or expertise
2. Specific management skills:
   - *Exercising good judgment:* the ability to plan and prepare for the future, respond to change, be held accountable for decisions made, and stay focused on objectives
   - *Organizing and coordinating:* the ability to organize tasks and their interdependent relationships
   - *Handling information:* using and communicating information
   - *Fostering personal growth and development:* encouraging both managers and employees to increase their knowledge and better themselves personally and professionally
   - *Handling conflict:* understanding the need for, and potential destructive force of, conflict

Take a look at the two lists again. Note that the emphasis of good management is placed on what a manager can *do* rather than what a manager knows. Yes, having specific expertise is often a precious commodity. But a good manager doesn't need to have a higher grade point average or more industrial experience than his or her subordinates. The ability to serve others, produce results, and get employees to do the same is what matters most.

Another Primary Managerial Skill:
Keeping Costs Down

Cutting costs refers to the practice of constantly striving to reduce a business's costs and using resources sparingly *without sacrificing quality.* From a manager's standpoint, the reason behind this is to create an atmosphere in which waste and excess are considered unacceptable. Wal-Mart is a good example of this practice. For instance, I've been told that it is Wal-Mart's policy to not provide its store managers with offices. Instead, every store's administrative staff shares a common work area. The absence of an office ensures that store managers walk the floor in a constant state of vigilance to ensure that everything is running smoothly. Just as important, eliminating offices keeps costs down. For the same reason no Wal-Mart manager can authorize payments above petty cash limits without first seeking approval from head office. It's also been reported that Wal-Mart managers are encouraged to take away free pens and other freebies when participating in training seminars and workshops. "For every dollar we save," the company keeps reminding its employees, "so too will our customers." Although such stringent measures might be considered draconian in other businesses, the clear message Wal-Mart sends out is that cutting costs is everyone's job. Perhaps a better way to successfully apply this concept is to make cutting *waste* a priority before hacking away at costs—costs that should have been kept to a minimum in the first place. Cutting too many costs almost always leads to a reduction in quality somewhere along the line, and that's just the tip of the iceberg. For an excellent article on how an obsession with cutting costs can lead to all sorts of "knock-on effect" problems, including company closures, job losses, and more, read the article "The Wal-Mart You Don't Know" by Charles Fishman (2003).

MANAGERIAL STYLES

How Does a Manager Obtain Results?

For many managers power is mostly wielded through trial and error. The style that worked best in the past is then dragged out and used again and again. There are probably as many management styles as there are streets in New York. Acclaimed management researcher Charles Handy has condensed the lion's share of these styles into six methods of influence:

1. *Force:* This is the crudest method. It is derived from pure authority and can range from outright threats to bullying.
2. *Rules and Procedures:* Setting down concrete rules and guidelines that everyone must follow is a time-honored way to control others. This is often the favored method of bureaucracies.
3. *Exchange:* Bargaining, negotiating, cajoling, and bribery fall under this category. Promotions, pay increases (bonuses), rewards, and recognition are more subtle examples.
4. *Persuasion:* This is usually the first method of choice. However, as Handy suggests, in practice it's usually contaminated by one of the other methods.
5. *Ecology:* This occurs when a manager uses his or her surroundings to exercise influence. The use of a crisis is a good example. (A colleague once relayed to me that in every job, most managers have three power-holding ecological moments: [1] when negotiating a contract, [2] during the first six months of employment, [3] during any moment of crisis.)
6. *Magnetism:* Sometimes witnessed in its abuse stages by salespeople, faith healers, religious fundamentalists, and so on. Personal charisma and obtaining followers are the keys to magnetism. (Handy, 1993)

One of the biggest dilemmas managers face is when to use these styles (or a variant thereof) to maximum benefit. Unfortunately, all succesful solutions are relative to the people involved and the situation encountered. What works for one manager may or may not work for another. What works one day may not work another. Therefore, instead of trying to establish a management cure-all (which doesn't exist), an emphasis should be placed on managers' choices and the consequences of those choices. For example:

- Using force or fear may achieve immediate results, but the results could be short-lived and lead to high employee turnover.
- Rules and procedures can effectively control behavior, but may drain a workplace of creativity, spontaneity, and morale.

- The exchange method can prove to be a good motivator, but can lead to problems when everyone expects some type of reward in exchange for doing a task. The result can be expensive, time consuming, and produce a lack of respect for management.
- With excessive use of the ecology method, managers might be seen as opportunistic or conniving.
- As for magnetism, well, as the expression goes, you can fool some of the people some of the time . . . but not all of the people all of the time.

So Which Style Is Best and When?

Management style theories tend to ebb and flow like tides, but one of the best (and one that I have personally used to great effectiveness) is known by the acronym MBWA (**m**anagement **b**y **w**alking **a**round). The idea behind MBWA is simple: to reduce the distance between manager and employee and strengthen the relationship (and understanding) between them. Just as the name suggests, MBWA demands that a manager get out of the office and walk around the shop floor. As acclaimed management consultant Richard Pascale explains, the point is not to interfere with employees but to draw management into reality (or, as he puts it, *get grounded*). Too often management lives and operates within its own perceptions of what is right or wrong rather than in what is real. The result manifests itself into various forms of misunderstanding, miscommunication, anger, and resentment. However, when contact between a manager and an employee is void of fear and apprehension, communication is strengthened. The result for the manager is a clearer understanding of what best motivates the employee, thereby suggesting a style of management that best suits the situation.

MBWA has other positive effects. It tends to reduce managerial arrogance as well as generate experience in influencing others. Not surprisingly, it's difficult to remain a liar or a control freak when face to face with employees every day. In addition, MBWA allows managers to see firsthand what's happening in their businesses without having it **filtered** by someone else. If what is seen is far enough out of line with what was previously believed, then management will be forced to update its thinking. That's when progress is made. Bear in mind that MBWA is not designed as a means of looking over employee's shoulders or becoming "the man who came to dinner." The idea is to facilitate cohesiveness, communication, cooperation, and improvement, and produce results.

TO RECAP

Good managers can be competent in a variety of fields if they posses above-average skills in (1) getting the most from employees, and (2) identifying (and acting upon) the needs and wants of internal and external customers. How a manager decides to handle this balancing act will result in a style or styles that greatly affect the business, the employees involved, and, most important, the paying customer.

Chapter 6

Getting the Most from Employees

In the About the Author on page *vi* of this book, much is made about the fact that I turned around three businesses. The statement is accurate, but in each of these businesses I probably came up with only a half dozen solutions to the seemingly infinite number of problems that were faced. The staff conceived the remaining ones. Yes, you read correctly—the *employees* had more to do with these business turnarounds than I did. As their manager I merely let them succeed—something none of my predecessors had allowed. Mind you, it took months to train these employees to be responsible (and brave) enough to solve their own work challenges, but after that mountain was climbed, situations improved in leaps and bounds. Simply put, as a manager I did not have a monopoly on intellect.

TAPPING INTO THE WORKFORCE

"Many hands make light work" says a popular proverb and the same can be said about many brains. Let's use a factory as an example. If employees are asked to clean and provide basic maintenance to their workstations on Mondays and Thursdays, they'll probably clean and provide basic maintenance to their workstations on Mondays and Thursdays. If a large order comes in on Tuesday and workstations become untidy, employees may wait until Thursday before attending to them. However, if they're told that *they alone are responsible* for ensuring that their workstations are *always* clean and well maintained, something different happens. By leaving the job up to the employees, their expertise and judgment has been applied.

Since most organizations are comprised of a number of employees, there are bound to be several interpretations of what constitutes an orderly workstation. Therefore the solution to ensuring that workstations remain appropriately clean and properly maintained depends on the organized transition of responsibility, outlined as follows:

Workstation Example	*Transitional Steps*
Informing employees of exactly what needs to be done	Creation of responsibility
Providing employees with relevant information	Training
Discussing with employees how they are to achieve their objective	Establishing work perimeters
Giving employees the tools necessary to accomplish their objective	Handing over authority
Reviewing the results	Enforcing accountability

Is it important to judge the method an employee uses to carry out a task? In certain cases yes—certain procedures must be followed due to safety and other factors. Otherwise, no. It's sometimes pointless to compare what an employee does with what a manager would have done in similar circumstances. In most cases a *result* is more important and should suit the task's purpose. In other words, if the solution is not contingent upon the process then the talents and abilities of employees should be left to their own accord. This is more than just a philosophical argument. If the right people were hired, trained accordingly, and provided with whatever is necessary to complete their jobs, then managers need to be extracting as much from these people as they can. The word for this is **delegation**.

DELEGATING RESPONSIBILITY

Delegation involves transferring a manager's decision-making authority and ability to act to a subordinate. The point is to get something done by someone else. This does not simply translate into assigning someone else to do a task. Delegation usually also allows employees to choose and implement *how* that task will be done. In doing so, an extraordinary sense of achievement is created. Delegation lets employees show the world what they are capable of accomplishing. Again, if the right people were hired to begin with then quite a lot should be accomplished.

To Delegate or Not to Delegate?

For most managers, delegation is not a choice. Most managers simply have more work than one person can be expected to perform. Thus the question is not whether one *should* delegate but *how*. Figuring out how can be quite intimidating. Perhaps the intimidation comes about when one imagines the negative consequence that can occur if an employee screws up a delegated task.

Taking the Fear Out of Delegation

As with most management subjects, the challenge behind delegation lies in its implementation. Many years ago I worked with a man who said that his father tried to teach him to swim by dragging him to a lake and throwing him in. He ended up thrashing around in the water before he was finally rescued. Ridiculous? Yes. But for many managers this "sink or swim" philosophy represents the very essence of how they delegate.

Another impedance to proper delegation is insecurity. Insecure managers don't trust others and often try and do everything themselves while complaining (or bragging) that they're overworked. Again, the result is that employees aren't used to their full potential. Here are some typical arguments used to avoid delegating:

> *Myth 1:* Delegation undermines a manager's position. Some managers believe that if tasks are routinely delegated to employees the employees will gain experience and skills, which will eventually enable them to steal their manager's job.
>
> *The Reality:* Good managers bolster their reputation and effectiveness by developing the people below them. Managers don't usually lose their jobs because they find and develop good people.

Myth 2: Because a manager is ultimately responsible for every delegated task, it's easier and safer for most managers to do everything they're responsible for themselves.

The Reality: A manager's time is limited. It's not possible for managers to do by themselves everything they're responsible for. Therefore, certain tasks and responsibilities *must* be handed to others.

Myth 3: A manager gives up power when delegating, thereby decreasing his or her effectiveness and authority.

The Reality: Delegation increases a manager's influence among employees. This enables most managers to widen their span of control, usually resulting in an increase in their powerbase.

Myth 4: Delegation demoralizes employees because most managers delegate the most boring tasks to their subordinates and leave the best stuff for themselves.

The Reality: Ironically, the fun tasks are usually the easiest to delegate. Besides, if managers chose to only do the fun things they wouldn't also be able to perform the tasks for which they alone are responsible.

Putting It All Together

Delegation need not be a fearful process. Using the following twelve steps should help eliminate most pitfalls:

1. *Don't assign duties because you don't want to perform them.* This includes managerial functions such as providing feedback, reprimanding, hiring and firing, training, motivating, handling sensitive issues, team-building, and so on.
2. *Clarify the assignment before it's delegated.* Determine what is being delegated, the results expected, and any time limitations. Again, unless specific methods must be adhered to, concentrate on the end results the employee must achieve instead of the means of doing so.
3. *Choose the right person for the right job.* Ensure that the employees have the time and motivation to complete it. Delegation, by its very nature, is designed to provide opportunities—not teach employees a lesson or put them in their place.

Know who is ready to handle more responsibility as well as how hard this person can be pushed.

4. *Determine work perimeters.* Let employees know *exactly* what they can and cannot do as well as what will make their job easier and any potentially damaging avenues they should avoid.

5. *Make delegation a gradual process by giving employees time to gain confidence.* The key is to provide employees with enough rope to be constructive without having them hang themselves. Ask yourself this: Can the task be done in stages?

6. *Discuss the tasks with the employees.* Allow employees to participate in discussions concerning what they are expected to do, how much authority they have, and by which standards they'll be judged. That way there will be fewer surprises in the end for both parties.

7. *Inform others about the delegation.* Failure to inform other employees of an impending delegation increases the likelihood of conflict and decreases the chance that the delegated task will be done efficiently.

8. *Allow the employees to make as many decisions as possible.* Unless your decisions are significantly better than the employees', let them use their own. Doing so is highly rewarding and deeply motivating for employees.

9. *Expect a mistake or two.* With appropriate monitoring you should be able to catch mistakes before they get out of hand. Remember that mistakes are a part of every learning process and tend to show at the very least that something is being done.

10. *Establish feedback controls.* Regular monitoring will help identify important problems or expensive mistakes at an early stage. Keep your office door open, but don't let this become a situation in which the employee is made to feel a constant, overshadowing presence. Let the employee know that help is available if needed or additional information/training is required (the catchy phrase for this is, "delegate don't abdicate").

11. *When problems arise, insist on solutions.* Along with ensuring that the employee does not feel abandoned, it is equally important that he or she does not keep running back to you with

each and every problem encountered. Insist that whenever a problem arises, the employee come to you with possible solutions rather than just the problem.

12. *Review results and reward good performance.* Let the employee know how he or she is doing. Praise any progress and politely address any setbacks. More often than not, people hunger for the chance to show how much they can accomplish. After employees have successfully completed a delegated task, act appropriately so that you can continue to get the most from your employees and ensure that they'll keep coming back for more.

THE EMPLOYEE-CUSTOMER CONNECTION

In the 1970s and early 1980s, the American car industry was in a crisis. How was an industry virtually invented by Americans brought to its knees? It's partly because when a rise in inflation and oil prices occured that dealt a massive one-two punch to every motor industry in the world, the administrators at the helm of the American car companies put their finance people in the driver's seat. Once the bean counters took control, they did their jobs wonderfully. Stopping financial losses became not only the end desire but also the means to achieving that end. Jobs were eliminated, production methods were squeezed, purchasing costs were reduced, new projects were canceled—everything was looked at through a microscope except the most important issue of all: what customers wanted in a car. However, the accountants can't be blamed. They did what they were supposed to do. They avoided risk. Accountants are supposed to steer a company away from all the attributes that can't be worked into a calculator. Intangibles such as innovation, style, and value were thrown to the wayside because they didn't fit into a ledger book. Time went by and employee morale decreased as the heart and spirit essential to manufacturing automobiles was smothered by the risk-free, concrete inflexibility of a finance company. Financial targets took priority and no one would listen to what those on the front lines (the dealers) had to say. Yet it was the car dealers who knew exactly what paying customers wanted, and who would eventually save the day.

Back to Basics (Again): Who's Most Important?

If external (paying) customers are the lifeblood of every business, then internal customers (employees) are its brain and muscle. Employees are the people who carry out the activities that make up an organization and ultimately determine a company's direction. Yet, before employees can, or will, work together, some sense of order and discipline must be established. Traditionally, this includes formulating a business **hierarchical pyramid** (see Figure 6.1).

The problem with this view, however, is that there's no room for external customers. It can probably be assumed that they're languishing somewhere below service-level employees. What would happen if a different approach were taken? What if management inverted this pyramid so that paying customers become the most important element? (See Figure 6.2.)

Showing a pyramid-shaped organizational chart from this perspective graphically displays the importance of the often disregarded service-level employee. In terms of who works for whom, it demonstrates that the group at the bottom should focus on providing for the group above. Every employee therefore shares a common purpose: to

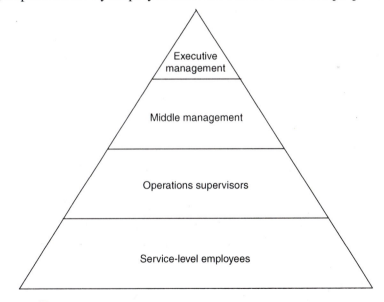

FIGURE 6.1. Traditional Business Hierarchical Pyramid

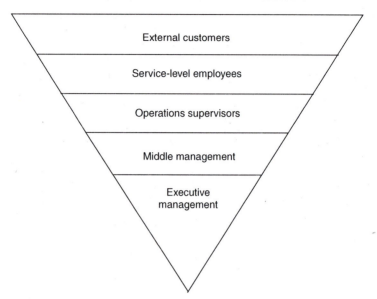

External customers

Service-level employees

Operations supervisors

Middle management

Executive
management

FIGURE 6.2. Inverted (or Customer-Oriented) Business Hierarchical Pyramid

work together to serve and satisfy his or her customers (a lesson lost on the car manufacturers' finance people).

Looking After Your People So That They'll Look After You

There's no doubt about it, the security, emotions, and well-being of employees have a direct effect on the service given to paying customers. Motivating employees becomes more difficult as employee numbers increase. Accepting the inverted hierarchical pyramid and the previously explained principles behind delegation are the first important steps in getting the most from employees, but they're only the first of many. In most organizations, different departments are constantly battling over territory. Each department is confident that their input and sense of direction is the most valid (as the finance people thought in the car industry). Within these departments, ambitious individuals are doing much the same thing. In fact, one of the greatest challenges of management lies in understanding that people are motivated for their *own* reasons, not a manager's reasons. In other words, ideas, rules, and regulations cannot be implemented unless the employees who must work with them *will* work with them. Thus, it is dependent on managers to provide employees with incentives for self-motivation. Years ago (and still today) this could be accomplished through fear. However, a better method is to go beyond delegation by allowing employees to make their own decisions and to some degree control their own destinations. This doesn't mean that everyone is allowed to go off in different directions. Strong leadership must be shown and it must be emphasized that employees will face the rewards or consequences of whatever they choose to do.

EMPLOYEE EMPOWERMENT

Transferring *ongoing* job-related authority and responsibility from management to workers is the way to **employee empowerment.** Similar to delegation, it's primarily done to motivate employees by allowing them to develop their own self-worth and, to some degree, operate with **autonomy.** The purpose of employee empowerment is to keep a company customer driven. First, management must start the process by (1) establishing clear, uncontested goals and guidelines, and (2) accepting that someone gaining power does not mean that someone else has to give it up.

Empowerment in Action

In Brazil, a country wracked by severe economic problems, one company keeps chugging along. Its name is Semco and it produces (among other things) turnkey biscuit factories, giant marine pumps, and industrial mixers that blend everything from rocket fuel to bubble gum. Before it acquired its fame, Semco suffered the usual rundown of corporate problems. Only after collapsing twice from stress-induced illnesses did CEO Ricardo Semler realize that something radical had to be done. In his book *Maverick* he describes how, over a period of several years, he gradually handed over his power and authority to company employees. This included allowing machine operators to lease Semco's expensive tools and machinery for their own purposes as well as assisting skilled employees to use the company's equipment and materials to set up their own businesses. Company executives at first derided this decision, predicting that chaos—or worse—would ensue. Semler thought differently. He began by teaching his workers accounting. This brought many to the previously inconceivable conclusion that the company's profits did not go straight into the bank accounts of top managers. They also learned to make their own decisions, quickly realizing that everyone ultimately benefited when the company did. Thus, workers were assured of job security if they prudently solved their own problems, cut waste, increased quality and production, worked together as a team, and weeded out laggards. Incredibly, employees grew so adept at this they eventually set their own salaries! In effect they had become the caretakers of the company that employed them and they alone became accountable for its success. Put simply, given a choice between success and failure, they chose success. Give a man a fish, suggests an age-old philosophy, and he has a meal. Teach him how to fish, and he will feed himself for the rest of his life.

Making Empowerment Work for You

How does a manager introduce the concept of empowerment? Obviously it doesn't happen overnight. It's a long process that demands strong leadership, honesty, cooperation, courage, and a commitment to serve. It necessitates cooperation from all involved as well.

For nonmanagers, empowerment means

- learning to take and handle responsibility (*warning:* be aware that some employees don't enjoy responsibility and prefer the safety of dead-end jobs);
- realizing that constant learning and training are a part of every job;
- understanding that the ownership of problems and solutions belongs to everyone in the business (i.e., problem prevention and work ownership);
- accepting that everyone needs to pull in the same direction (i.e., serve others);
- showing up for work and performing bottom-line duties is not enough—wages are given for value created; and
- displaying caring, integrity, and trust.

For managers, empowerment involves

- viewing workers as assets (not expenditures) and recognizing their value;
- sharing information and providing good training;
- listening, asking, valuing, and then acting on other's viewpoints and ideas;
- creating a motivating environment conducive to creativity, participation, and innovation;
- working toward preventing problems—not just battling them;
- rewarding good performance;
- displaying caring, integrity, and trust;
- prudently choosing the right people for the right jobs; and
- ensuring that employees and departments serve each other (pull in the same direction).

Another, Simpler Example

Years ago, a well-known retail operation in the United States watched its sales plummet. Managers blamed it on the faltering economy, yet in the same area of the country another retail operation prospered. Investigations later revealed that the first retailer used an employee manual the size and thickness of a phone book. In militant detail it dictated to employees how to think, dress, behave, and carry out their duties. The second retailer had a different approach. Its employee manual is written on a single 5 × 8 inch card that reads:

Welcome to Our Company. We're glad to have you with us.
Our number one goal is to *provide outstanding customer service.*
Set your personal and professional goals high; we have great confidence in your abilities.

Our Rules:

Rule 1. Use your good judgment in all situations.

There will be no additional rules.
(Please feel free to approach the department manager, store manager, or division manager if you have any questions at any time.)

If you're still not convinced that empowerment works, ask yourself the following questions: (1) Which of these companies would you rather work for, the first or the second? and (2) Do you think that allowing employees to use their own judgment means that management has lost control, or gained it?

SUMMARY

Delegation involves assigning an employee a specific responsibility and having that person use his or her talents to successfully complete it. In other words, delegation is task related. Empowerment goes beyond that. Empowerment is an ongoing process that involves the *complete* transfer of job-related authority and responsibility from managers to workers. With delegation there is a foreseeable end to an assigned task. Empowerment has no end. Once a goal (such as providing 100 percent satisfaction to customers) has been established, it's up to the employee to march toward it and keep marching toward it. Both *delegation and empowerment are designed to motivate employees* by allowing them to show others what they can do, to be creative, and seek out their own sense of fulfillment. However the onus is upon the manager to set the stage for success by taking these steps:

1. *Assigning responsibility.* Explain exactly what needs to be done as well as any work perimeters.
2. *Granting authority to act.* Spend money, direct the work of others, use resources, and so on.
3. *Creating accountability.* Have the worker agree to become directly obligated to the task as well as be responsible for any outcomes and performance results.
4. *Not abandoning (or abdicating) his/her position.* Management's office door is kept open to any problems, concerns, or needs.
5. *Maintaining trust.* Like freedom, once empowerment has been bestowed upon people it cannot be taken away without repercussions. When employees have shown that they can handle responsibility they should be congratulated and directed toward other endeavors. Only then can a manager truly begin to
   • reduce his or her workload,
   • tap into the company workforce,
   • create an atmosphere of problem prevention and personal responsibility (work ownership), and
   • provide the ultimate in human motivation.

Chapter 7

Organizational Structures and Cultures

BUREAUCRATIC AND ADAPTIVE ORGANIZATIONS

Organizational structure refers to how a firm is organized. In graphic terms, this means how the chain of command is arranged in a hierarchical pyramid. Diagramming a business in this manner shows how its entities are tied together and, in part, how information moves (or doesn't move) within it. Generally speaking, there are two kinds of business structures: **bureaucratic** (or mechanistic) **organizations** and **adaptive** (or organic) **organizations**. Bureaucratic (mechanistic) organizations thrive in stable environments. Adaptive (organic) organizations do best in dynamic or rapidly changing environments.

Figure 7.1. dramatically illustrates why the process of going from a bureaucratic organizational structure to an adaptive one—as most current management trends are designed to do—is often referred to as *flattening* an organization. Flat organizations have fewer layers of management that are replaced by autonomous (empowered) employees. Fewer managers and fewer chain-of-command restrictions create an environment that increases managerial responsibility. The idea behind creating an organization such as this is twofold: (1) autonomous employees can react to changes in the marketplace faster when fewer managers, fewer piles of paperwork, and fewer rules and regulations stand in their way; and (2) flat organizations bring managers (and everyone else) closer to their customers. Figure 7.2 showcases the differences between bureaucratic and adaptive organizations.

Which organizational structure is best? That depends on a business's nature and needs. The ultimate purpose of organizational design is to put into place a structure that enables the implementation and achievement of key goals and objectives. Some employees enjoy the safe, slow pace, the comfort of rules and regulations, and the from-the-top-down authority of bureaucracies (probably because bu-

A Bureaucratic-Type Organization

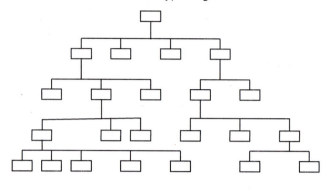

An Adaptive-Type Organization

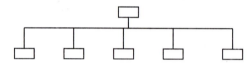

FIGURE 7.1. Comparison of Bureaucratic and Adaptive Organization Diagrams

reaucracies discourage risk or performance above the norm). Others thrive on the freedom, constant changes, and ability to make decisions inherent in adaptive organizations. Many business practitioners (and academics) advocate the flexibility and speed inherent in adaptive organizational structures.

The IBM Story

Business tales are notorious for being so full of hyperbole that it's often difficult to separate fact from fiction, but the lessons they generate are usually reason enough to repeat them. One case in point, and a good way to bring to life the importance of organizational structure and culture, is the story behind how IBM, who invented the first office computer, developed its first personal computer for use at home.

Prior to the development of the world's first personal computer (PC), IBM was a large and powerful corporation. Affectionately referred to as "Big Blue," it dominated the international business ma-

Bureaucratic organizations (mechanistic design)		Adaptive organizations (organic design)
Centralized (power comes from the top)	**Authority** →	Decentralized (employee empowerment)
Many	**Rules and procedures** →	Few
Small	**Span of control** (the number of people reporting to a manager) →	Large
Specialized	**Tasks** →	Shared
Few	**Teams and task forces** →	Many
Formal and impersonal	**Coordination** →	Informal and personal

FIGURE 7.2. Bureaucratic and Adaptive Organization Policy Spectrum (*Source:* Adapted from Burns and Stalker [1994]. *The Management of Innovation.* Oxford: Oxford University Press.)

chine market. Yet when the personal computer was invented and began demonstrating its potential, IBM famously decided to ignore this "fad" and stick to manufacturing typewriters, calculators, and adding machines. In fact many years earlier the CEO of IBM had publicly proclaimed that computers were a dead-end market because the world would only ever need five or six of them! Of course by the time IBM realized this wasn't the case, it was too late. Like a giant ocean liner the IBM bureaucracy was so intransigent and colossal (for instance, a great deal of effort was spent enforcing a strict dress and behavioral code) it simply couldn't change its course quickly. As a result, dozens of smaller companies sprang up, each taking advantage of the rapidly expanding home-computer market.

In desperation, IBM's top administrators gathered together a team of the company's best people and sent them to Florida to design a marketable home computer. As legend has it, freed from the company's binding bureaucracy, they designed the IBM personal computer in record time. Unfortunately, when these people returned to their posts they were once again chained to the same unyielding rules and procedures that had prevented IBM from developing a home computer in the first place. As a result, every one of them quit the company within a year. IBM did, of course, survive thanks to its new PC, but by then too many competitors had entered the market and as a result it never regained the reputation or market share it once enjoyed. It has since dedicated itself to becoming flatter.

ORGANIZATIONAL CULTURES

In continuing with the theme of organizational structure, it's important to note that every business also has its own unique culture, which dictates to some degree, either by rule or example, the way the business is organized, how people think, and how things are done. This is called **organizational culture**. The culture a business practices is defined as a system of shared values held by an organization that distinguishes its methods of operation from others. These methods include the following:

- *Innovation and risk taking:* the level to which employees are encouraged to take risks and/or do new things

- *Attention to detail:* the degree to which employees are expected to exhibit precision and/or analysis in their work
- *Outcome orientation:* whether management focuses more on results and outcomes or on the techniques and processes to achieve those outcomes
- *People orientation:* the importance the organization places on its people
- *Team organization:* the degree to which an emphasis is placed on teams rather than individuals
- *Aggressiveness:* the level of "hunger" and competitiveness that exists within the organization
- *Stability:* the emphasis placed on maintaining the status quo in contrast to growth

Subcultures

In many organizations, usually larger ones, there also exist **subcultures.** These are found in different departments, branches, and/or work groups. Subcultures operate similar to organizational cultures but on a smaller scale. For example, the precision and formality of an accounting department usually induces operating under a stricter system than the looseness, innovation, and creativity needed in a product design department. To accomplish their goals and develop their people, each department must establish its own distinct rules and procedures (culture) in order to facilitate success.

Cultural Classifications

There are probably as many different organizational cultures as there are organizations, but in 1972, management researcher Roger Harrison identified four distinct types. Again, the type of culture a business establishes should be contingent upon the product or service it offers and what it hopes to achieve. Harrison's designations are as follows:

1. The *power culture* is based on key individuals who generate control from their center. There are few rules and little bureaucracy. Power cultures can move quickly and react well (if they are inclined to); however, if key individuals are removed the or-

ganization is extremely vulnerable to collapse. (Examples of this include companies with celebrity CEOs, companies for which the CEO either invented or innovated the product, or, in general, any company in which the CEO has high levels of control.)

2. The *role culture* is rigid and formal, often stereotyped as bureaucracy, although not always in its negative sense. Coordination is maintained by a narrow band of senior management. Performance above and beyond the established guidelines is not needed. Personal power is frowned upon. Rules and procedures are the major methods of influence. (Examples of this include the military, government, and large corporations.)

3. The *task culture* is project oriented. The emphasis is on getting the job done. Attention is given to skills, and to putting the right people in the right job and letting them get on with it. Task cultures are results-oriented and usually very adaptable. They tend to thrive where creativity, competitiveness, and speed are required. (Examples of this include advertisement teams, computer software developers, construction contractors, etc.)

4. The *person culture* has the individual as the center point. Person-culture organizations exist because the people within them are doing their own thing yet still pulling in the same direction. (Examples of this include lawyers, physicians, university professors, etc.) (Harrison, 1972)

Where Does Company Culture Come From?

Company culture can derive from a number of sources, but the three important ones follow:

1. *The environment.* Whether in the city or the countryside, landlocked or on the sea, a business's location can have a profound influence on culture. A country, its customs, technology, the levels of available education, local and national politics, the economy, even climate can influence human interaction and development. The result is a marked influence on organizational culture. For example, when I was working on my bachelor's degree at Florida State University I had a roommate from New York City who took as many classes as he could fit into his schedule. His idea was to graduate quickly and head back to

New York. When I asked him why, he said he couldn't bear the thought of slowing down. "And if I stay here too long that's exactly what's going to happen!" he insisted. He firmly believed that people in Florida (or the entire southern United States for that matter) were too laid back. "If I get back to the rush and bustle of New York and I've become a Floridian," he told me, "I'll be eaten alive!"

2. *Leadership (and in particular, company founders).* When it comes to establishing company priorities or setting a work ethic, the influence of a business leader can last for an organization's lifetime. For example, Ray Kroc of McDonald's fame didn't found the company, but his legendary obsession with hygiene and cleanliness exists long after his death. Today, regardless of what you think of the food, it's difficult to fault the high sanitary standards of most McDonald's restaurants.

3. *Past successes or failures.* How a company treats its successes is equally as important as how it behaves when it fails. A good example of this is reflected in Coca-Cola's disastrous decision in the 1980s to change its centuries-old formula. The vice president who initiated this change (and conducted the $4 million in research that supported it) was a lifetime employee who had worked his way to the top of the company the hard way. Coca-Cola was his life, but his decision was nevertheless a bad one. Pepsi, Coke's biggest competitor, pounced on the change, claiming that it meant something was wrong with the original formula and that it was being altered to more closely mimic Pepsi. Whether Pepsi was right or wrong is irrelevant; the result was that Coke's market share plummeted. Desperate to stop its hemorrhaging, the company reintroduced its old formula and fired the vice president who had instigated the change. Morale at Coca-Cola reportedly went south as employees came to the realization that new ideas (and the mistakes that sometimes result from them) were not tolerated. Seven years later, a newly appointed CEO rehired the vice president. The intended message was to let employees know that moving forward meant taking risks—and that mistakes, as long as they're learned from, are acceptable. (It wouldn't be surprising if the CEO also realized that of all the people in the world who had the least chance

of making another mistake of epic proportions, it was that vice president!)

The Two Levels of Organizational Culture

In every business, culture exists on two separate levels. The first is **observable culture,** or what one sees and hears when walking around the company's premises. This includes:

- *Stories:* the tales told again and again about dramatic incidents within the company
- *Heroes:* the people singled out for special attention (and whose stories are told again and again)
- *Rites and rituals:* ceremonies, meetings, and celebrations (e.g., the annual company award banquet)
- *Symbols:* the use of language or nonverbal expressions to communicate important themes (An example of this is reflected in the Polish university where I began teaching. The corridors are lined with photographs of presidents, prime ministers, Nobel Laureates, and other people of distinction—all of whom have taught or spoken at the school. Other examples include corporate logos, charity funding, public relations campaigns, and even architecture.)

The second level of a business's culture is unseen. This is called the **core culture,** and it reflects the values or underlying beliefs that influence employee behavior. Examples include:

- *Performance excellence* (the way employees are judged)
- *Innovation* (if or how new ideas are welcomed)
- *Social responsibility* (the importance placed on environmental and social ethics)
- *Worker involvement* (the level to which employees are involved in decision making)
- *Quality of work life* (the state of general working conditions)

How Is Company Culture Maintained?

Culture is usually maintained in three no-nonsense ways:

1. Hiring people who think the way management does and firing those who do not (e.g., some organizations make candidates go through as many as twelve interviews before being selected).
2. Indoctrination (the types and levels of employee training).
3. Having management set an example.

Strong versus Weak Organizational Cultures

Culture plays a significant role in a company's work climate. Strong cultures often influence the behavior of employees more than weak cultures because a high degree of shared values tends to create an atmosphere of control. In other words, if more employees accept a company's values the company's culture, as well as its influence on employees, will be stronger.

A good way to demonstrate this is with Disney World in Orlando, Florida. Disney World has an extraordinarily strong culture. Apart from the lingo (uniforms are called *costumes,* employees are *cast members,* being at work is considered being *on stage,* and so on), employees are told what color underwear to wear, how much jewelry can be worn, the type of hairstyles allowed, the intensity of perfume or cologne, and many other restrictions. The purpose of this is to establish a strict "Disney look" and ensure unity. It sounds awful, but the company balances these rather militant demands with a welcoming attitude that's hard to beat. On my first day at work there (all new employees attend two days of Disney University prior to beginning their jobs), the manager in charge of training cheerfully announced, "Welcome to Disney World! I want you to know that for every person sitting in this room more than 200 applicants were turned down. Why? Because we wanted *you!*"

No company had ever said that to me before and it made me (and everyone else) feel very good. I was ready to toe the line.

Of course that doesn't mean strong cultures are for everyone. The days are long gone when IBM employees had to stand beside their desks each morning and sing the corporate anthem, but some companies still vigorously encourage unity and high morale via similar actions (something that tends to be accepted more readily in America than in other countries). Having workers stand in a circle while clapping and chanting uplifting slogans ("We're number one, we're number one") is but one example. Personally, I'd rather have needles stuck in my eyes. However, if employees respond to this style of morale building, then it's certainly worth doing.

CAN STRUCTURE AND CULTURE BE CHANGED?

Organizational structure and culture are powerful manipulators of employee behavior and success, but what if they adversely affect a company? How can an organization's culture be changed into something more suitable? Although some people feel that it's easier to work within a company's culture rather than try to change it, the issue of change, which can be applied to organizational structure and culture, is nevertheless addressed in the next chapter.

Chapter 8

Managing Change

There is nothing more difficult to take in hand, more perilous to conduct, or more uncertain in its success than to take the lead in the introduction of a new order of things.

Machiavelli

In words difficult to improve upon, writer Bruce Chatwin once suggested that a fundamental contributor to all-around good health is experiencing **change**. "Diversion, distraction, fantasy, change of food, fashion, love and landscape; we need them as the air we breathe," he wrote. "Without change our bodies rot. The man who sits quietly in a shuttered room is likely to be mad—tortured by hallucinations and introspection" (Chatwin, 1996).

Chatwin went on to say that changes of scenery and the passage of seasons have been proven to stimulate the rhythms of the brain as well as contribute to a sense of well-being and an active purpose in life:

Monotonous surroundings weave patterns that produce fatigue, nervous disorders, apathy, self-disgust, and violent reactions. It is hardly surprising then, that generations cushioned from the cold by central heating, from the heat by air-conditioning, and carted in aseptic transports from one identical house or hotel to another, should feel the need for journeys of mind or body, for pep pills or tranquilizers, or for the cathartic journeys of sex, music and dance. We spend far too much time in shuttered rooms. (Chatwin, 1996)

It's tough to argue with this sentiment, yet, ironically, although change is inevitable and indeed necessary, when it comes to management, it's almost always resisted.

In his book, *Management: Theory and Practice,* author Gerald Cole sums up the change process well. To change something, he says, implies altering it, varying it, or modifying it in some way. Some organizations change mainly in response to external circumstances **(reactive change)**; others change principally because they have decided to change **(proactive change).** Some businesses are conservative in outlook, seeking little in the way of change; others are entrepreneurial in outlook, always seeking new opportunities and new challenges. Some organizations are constructed in such a way that change and/or adaptation is a slow and difficult process. Others are designed with built-in flexibility—enabling adaptation to take place regularly and relatively easily. There is not much point in change for change's sake, and most people need to be persuaded of the need for change. The reality is that every group has forces within it that keep it together and provide it with stability and others that provide it with reasons to change and adapt.

PREPARING FOR ORGANIZATIONAL CHANGE

For too many companies the buzzwords *reengineering, restructuring,* and *downsizing* are the only methods of change. Unfortunately these methods of change usually amount to little more than laying off scores of employees. Saving money by eliminating workers is a timeless act, but it shouldn't be the sole device of organizational change. Besides, the practice of casting adrift large numbers of employees often returns to haunt a business. Imagine the captain of a ship eliminating a large number of his crew to enable his provisions to last longer. Sure, he'll save money, but when the first storm hits (as storms eventually do) his ship will most assuredly suffer because there aren't enough people on board to sail it.

Introducing change into a business, therefore, should be a *proactive process that focuses on customer needs.* This includes

- cutting waste,
- reducing customer waiting time,
- increasing product or service quality,

- eliminating unnecessary paperwork, and
- generally streamlining operations to serve customers better.

In order for *effective* change to be implemented and take hold within an organization **breadth** and **depth** are required. *Breadth* means that change must take place across the entire organization (i.e., every department and area from the executive offices to the stockroom). *Depth* means that everyone within these departments must be aware of why change is occurring and *be involved* in the change process. Getting employees involved in change (having them become part owners in the process by asking for their input) is a powerful way to win them over. Yet, for many, the fears that changes bring are valid. These fears include job loss, embarrassment at not being able to adapt to new technologies or new practices, and so forth. The result usually manifests itself into some form of resistance—either seen or otherwise.

UNDERSTANDING RESISTANCE TO CHANGE

Probably the Most Important Management Theory Ever Developed

In the 1950s Kurt Lewin developed a model (the Force-Field Theory) that helps explain organizational change and its resistance (see Figure 8.1). Lewin states that there are two forces at work in change situations. The first comes from those who are trying to instigate change *(driving forces)*. The second results from those who are resisting it *(restraining forces)*.

Lewin says that most people prefer to use force (or power) to bring about change. This means that they try to "win" by exerting pressure on those who oppose them. In practice, though, the more one side pushes the more the other pushes back. Therefore, the better way of overcoming resistance is to concentrate on the removal or weakening of the objections and fears of the opposing side. The question management should be asking isn't "How can we persuade these people of our arguments for change?" but rather, "What are their objections and fears and how can we deal with them?"

Restraining forces

(forces resisting change)

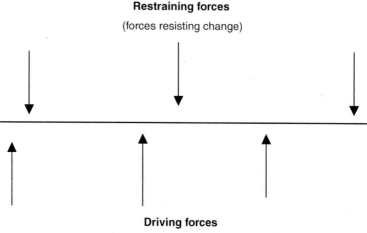

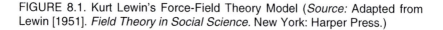

Driving forces

(forces for change)

FIGURE 8.1. Kurt Lewin's Force-Field Theory Model (*Source:* Adapted from Lewin [1951]. *Field Theory in Social Science.* New York: Harper Press.)

Understanding Human Nature

Initiating change can be such a gut-wrenching experience that it's been known to reduce seasoned executives to tears. This is because the comfort of old habits and protective barriers are broken down and rearranged during the change process, leaving everyone feeling stranded and fighting for their professional lives. The following text is adapted from *Creating Value for Customers* by William Band. It adequately explains the feelings a business is likely to encounter when dealing with change:

- *Fear of loss of control:* People feel that things are being done *to* them rather than *by* them.
- *Too much uncertainty:* The future is not obvious, and every day feels like walking off a cliff. This can lead to people wanting excessive details, contingency plans, and other procrastination techniques (i.e., paralysis by analysis).
- *Too many surprises:* People like novelty, but hate surprises. Early warnings are necessary to avoid unwanted shocks.

- *Letting go of habits:* Habits are efficient, effective, and mindless. Change will be uncomfortable.
- *Need for familiarity:* Everybody likes what is familiar. We feel comfortable going to places and doing things we are familiar with.
- *Fear of more work:* True, implementing new ideas means more work, especially at the beginning of change, but this often subsides, and tasks can become easier and more efficient (usually the reason for change).
- *Concern for competence:* People often question their ability to master new skills, particularly if training and ongoing support are not provided or are viewed with skepticism.
- *Time to adjust:* Saying "Let's do things differently" is not enough. It takes time for new skills and a sense of comfort to develop. Rushing through the change process can lead to disruption, sabotage, foot-dragging, and poor performance. (Bard, 1991)

BUILDING THE COMMITMENT TO CHANGE

With Kurt Lewin's Force-Field Theory in mind, there are seven ways a manager can reduce the fears that change creates:

1. *Involve as many people as possible.* Participation leads to ownership, enthusiasm, and motivation.
2. *Communicate clearly and often.* Provide as much information as possible.
3. *Divide changes into manageable, comprehensive steps.* Make these steps as familiar as possible and make them small and easy. Also, ensure each step is deemed a success.
4. *Never surprise anyone with change.*
5. *Let commitment grow.* Don't ask for immediate allegiance to new and untried ways (you won't get it).
6. *Make clear what will be expected of people during and after the change.* Communicate standards and requirements.
7. *Provide as much continuous training as needed.*

Change from Another Angle

In 1952, Kurt Lewin developed a Three Stage Approach to Change Behavior that was later elaborated upon by Edgar Schein in 1969. Since good habits are recognized as being just as difficult to break as bad ones, Lewin makes the analogy of unfreezing (or breaking) bad habits and then freezing good habits once they've been established:

1. *Unfreeze existing behaviors.* Gain acceptance for change by reducing fear.
2. *Change existing behaviors.* Implement change through breadth, depth, and work ownership.
3. *Freeze new behaviors.* Reinforce new patterns of thinking and working via rewards and praise. (*Note:* if this is not done, employees *will* revert to their old ways.)

Remember: Different Strokes for Different Folks

No solution to change is all-encompassing. In 1996, Paul Strebel, working out of the Institute of Management Development in Lausanne, Switzerland, came up with a diagram (modified in Figure 8.2) that demonstrates that one, never-fail solution does not exist. Instead, there are many.

Strebel's point is that every type of situation that requires change is different. Therefore, managers cannot expect to blindly apply a one-size-fits-all strategy. In the diagram I've labeled the boxes with numbers 1 through 9. The greater the number, the more drastic are the actions needed to implement change. For example, managing a crisis in the face of strong forces against change (box 9) often requires radical action (firing people), which is completely different from trying to stimulate change when things are going well (box 1).

CHANGE MANAGEMENT: SOME EXAMPLES

A Personal Look

When I entered business school I'd just completed my second business turnaround and had found the experience excruciating. Naturally, because it had been so difficult (much more difficult than my

Type of change

	Proactive	Active	Rapid
High resistance to change	7 Radical leadership (charisma)	8 Reassigning people and responsibilities	9 Eliminating jobs and/or people
Medium resistance to change	4 Management-led changes	5 Redesigning of processes	6 Autonomous restructuring
Low resistance to change	1 Employee-led changes	2 Goal setting (creating incentives to make changes)	3 Rapid adaptation to change
	Weak	Moderate	Strong

**Perceived need to adapt to change
(change force)**

FIGURE 8.2. Paul Strebel's Change Willingness Grid (*Source:* Adapted from Strebel [1996]. Choosing the Right Change Path. *The Financial Times,* 14 [February]: 5.)

first turnaround, which involved little more than setting improved quality standards for a half dozen highly skilled technicians in a television studio—something they readily agreed to undertake), I thought I'd done a number of things wrong. After looking into the matter, however, it became apparent that few, if any, business turnarounds are easy. In fact, it was shocking to learn that I'd actually done most things right. More astonishing was finding out that many business turnaround successes, as with mine, are not the result of a master plan. Concentrating on formulating and carrying out plans too easily leads to restrictive procedures that can suffocate the change process. Instead, when it comes to implementing change, most successful managers (as business guru Richard Pascale says) set out into the unknown with the heart of an explorer and the mind of a business contractor, armed with common sense, a basic understanding of their business and customers, and an overwhelming desire to excel.

Does This Stuff **Really Work?**

Perhaps the best testimonial I can offer comes from an executive earning his MBA through a postgraduate program I was helping to teach in Europe. Change management was one of the first subjects I introduced when my section of the program began. At our next meeting several weeks later, the executive stood and announced, "That change management stuff is fantastic! I've been using it at work and believe it or not it produced results. No kidding." He stopped and laughed. "Imagine that," he continued, "we've finally learned something in an MBA program we can actually use!"

Chapter 9

Managing Conflict

In the 1980s, management gurus Tom Peters and Robert Waterman published a book titled *In Search of Excellence: Lessons from America's Best-Run Companies.* The book immediately stormed onto the best-seller lists. It became one of the top sellers of all time, racking up sales of more than 8 million copies. Basically, *In Search of Excellence (ISoE)* examined some of the most successful businesses in America and identified eight common traits, which are explained as follows:

1. *They were action oriented.* Management placed an emphasis on production and performance (i.e., made things happen).
2. *They were close to their customers.* Each sold what customers wanted to buy rather than what the business wanted to sell. In order to do this, the business listened to their customers and then created an environment that could deliver what their customers wanted.
3. *They were autonomous and entrepreneurial.* To a certain degree, each business let its employees call the shots. In doing so employees tried new things and took measured risks.
4. *They believed that productivity came through people.* Each business operated under the concept that if people are treated well, they will reciprocate in kind.
5. *Managers had a hands-on, value-driven style.* Managers didn't sit in an ivory tower and they didn't consider nonmanagement employees to be beneath them.
6. *Each business stuck to what it knew best.* As a rule, most companies didn't diversify into areas in which they knew nothing.
7. *Each organization had a lean staff.* Each business tended to adapt a flat organization structure (no bureaucracy, red tape, or

top-heavy management structure). Also, communication chan-
nels were clear and accessible.

8. *They each had simultaneous loose-tight properties.* Autonomy
was given to employees on the shop floor, yet each business was
firmly "grounded" and committed to its core values.

Of course many companies, when studied, claim that they're doing
everything right, but about ten years after *ISoE* was released, one of
its contributors (Richard Pascale) decided to take another look at the
companies he and his colleagues had studied to see how they were
doing. What he found shocked him. About two-thirds had lost huge
amounts of market share. Several appeared on the verge of bankruptcy. What in the world had gone wrong?

On a side note, it's interesting to mention what happened when this
information surfaced. Human nature being what it is, *ISoE* was derided, sneered at, and attacked by almost every business writer and
academic that had failed to make the best-seller lists (and many more
to boot). It's a shame because *ISoE* is a well-written book that makes
many valid claims.

The problem for the companies examined in *ISoE* was that they
had probably taken too much of a good thing and gone overboard—
not unlike a person who is issued a drug prescription to take one pill
every 24 hours and decides to take the whole bottle under the assumption that it will induce recovery faster, or a person who decides to lose
weight and becomes anorexic. In addition, in a slash-and-burn fervor
to become lean and mean, many of the companies had effectively
eliminated one ingredient crucial to every business's success: **conflict.**

THE VALUE OF CONFLICT

The Best Business Story Ever

The quality of Honda products is legendary, but who would ever
believe that this quality was born out of conflict? The Honda Motor
Company has been listed as one of the best-managed companies in
the world for so long that few people take notice of it anymore, and
even fewer remember the company's dramatic history. One of the sto-

ries behind the company's success (which I'm sure has inflated over the years) rarely fails to reduce an audience to utter silence.

As a young man, the company's founder, Soichiro Honda, had a fascination with small engines and motorbikes. Keep in mind that this was in the days following World War II. As a Japanese man, Honda had huge obstacles to overcome. Yet, despite these setbacks, his reputation for producing engines of superior quality grew. Beside him every step of the way stood Takeo Fujisawa, a man who became Honda's longtime friend and business partner. Success followed success until Honda decided that the future of motors lay with air-cooled engines. His partner disagreed, insisting that water-cooled engines were the only way to go. Thus began a disagreement of epic proportions. Eventually, the two men could no longer work together because of their arguments. "It's my company, we're going with air-cooled engines, and that's final!" Honda shouted. As a result, Fujisawa stormed out of the company and quit. Sometime later, Honda came to the sobering realization that the future of the combustion engine did indeed lay with water-cooled engines—and that he had driven away the only person in his company who had the guts to tell him so. Aghast at what he'd done, he went to find his friend. As legend has it—and here's where the story starts sounding biblical—he eventually found him in a monastery; apparently, Fujisawa was so angry he was considering becoming a monk. Honda then did two of the most astonishing things any company CEO has probably ever done. (1) He apologized and admitted he'd been wrong, and (2) he vowed that from then on he was going to create a company in which *anyone* would be able to look their boss in the face and say, "You're wrong" without suffering any consequences.

Think about it. Soichiro Honda worked during a time when *nobody* in any Japanese company dared question his superior. Yet he decided to break away from this accepted way of thinking (as well as popular hierarchical business practices) and create a work environment that embraced the one thing that almost everyone tries to avoid with a passion. Soichiro Honda wanted a company that welcomed, and in many instances *encouraged,* conflicts. By doing so, he felt that his employees would forever be able to safely question one another, thereby helping to eliminate any future bad decisions.

THE NATURE OF WORK-RELATED CONFLICT

Major Truths Behind Conflict

Why is handling conflict important? As the Honda case shows, having everyone toe the company line can result in disaster—particularly when the company is heading for a cliff. There are other reasons as well. According to the American Management Association, 20 percent of a manager's time is spent dealing with conflict situations. That's one out of every five hours. With this in mind, here are some important points to remember:

- Not all conflicts are worth a manager's time and effort (conflicts can be trivial).
- Some conflicts are unmanageable (they may be outside management's sphere of influence, or the involved parties may not be interested in a resolution).
- Conflicts have causes (they don't spring up out of thin air). So it's in management's best interests to dig for the sources of disagreement and know the players. What are their interests, feelings, values, and personalities?

Major Causes of Work-Related Conflict

Most work-related conflicts do not transpire into open dramatics or fistfights. Instead, they fester under a thin veil of civility that invisibly consumes energy, productivity, and money. Beginning the process of conflict resolution involves accepting that solutions tend to fall into two categories: *cooperating* (the desire to satisfy another person) and *assertiveness* (the desire to satisfy the self). First, it's important to ascertain what type of conflict exists. Types of conflict are as follows:

> *Communicative conflict* results from misunderstandings or crossed wires (but not, as many people believe, a lack of communication, because in most conflicts a lot of "talking" is going on).
> *Substantive (structural) conflict* involves differences in goals, allocation of resources, distribution of rewards, policies and procedures, and job assignments.

Emotional (personal) conflict results from feelings of anger, distrust, dislike, fear, resentment, and personality clashes.

Two Directions Conflict Can Take

Conflict can make or break a business depending on how employees perceive it. With **dysfunctional conflict,** everyone either avoids or sadistically prepares for the imminent confrontation of those with opposing views. Issues are constantly seen as black or white, or right or wrong. The result, more often than not, is that tempers run high, battles erupt, and employees end up canceling each other out.

With **functional conflict,** people have been trained to respect opposing views and agree not to be threatened by them (suggestions on how to do this are mentioned in the next chapter). Establishing a company culture that can cope with disagreement in the form of functional conflict helps emphasize the importance of individual input and creativity. Conflicts can then take the form of civilized (if not animated) discussion, thereby clearing the air and lowering an organization's collective blood pressure. In other words, disagreement does not mean that war has been declared. Instead, employees learn to express their views without attacking others, and to listen to others without taking offense.

DEALING WITH CONFLICT

Typical Options Taken When Conflict Arises

Following is a list of options we've all resorted to at one time or another when trying to handle conflict. Which method best suits the needs of your internal or external customers?

1. *Avoidance:* best used when the conflict is trivial, when emotions are running high, or when attempts at resolution can be more disruptive than the conflict itself.
2. *Accommodation:* placing another's needs or interests ahead of one's own. **Accommodation** is useful when the issue under dispute is not of great interest to you or if you need to build up credits for later use.

3. *Forcing:* getting your way at the expense of another. Forcing your views on others becomes necessary when a quick resolution is needed, when unpopular actions must be taken, or when commitment by others is not critical.
4. *Compromise:* requires each party to give up something of value. Usually compromise can only be used when all parties are of equal power, when time pressures are being felt, or when a temporary solution is needed for a complex problem.
5. *Collaboration:* ends in a win-win solution for all parties. This can only occur when honesty, trust, and empathy are an integral part of discussions.

Making Conflict Work for You: Conflict Stimulation

Functional conflict is healthy and stimulating, but, again, employees must be trained in its implementation before it can produce results. It should be introduced in these situations:

1. When subordinates believe it's in their best interests to maintain the appearance of peace and cooperation (i.e., when "yes-men" dominate)
2. When employees show high resistance to change
3. When there is a general lack of ideas in the business
4. In a business that has unusually low employee turnover and/or an emphasis is placed on maintaining the status quo

Playing with Dynamite (or How to Stimulate Conflict)

1. *Tossing communicative grenades.* When things need to get moving quickly, one way of lighting a fire under everyone is to state something ambiguous (money is being lost, two departments are merging, people are going to be laid off), or send out a nasty memo and wait for the reaction. Be careful with this though. You may be the one who ends up getting burned.
2. *Bringing in outsiders.* Bringing in people whose backgrounds, values, attitudes, and styles are different often helps shake things up.
3. *Restructuring.* Reassigning jobs and responsibilities can really get the ball rolling. This is vividly displayed in governmental cabinet reshuffles.

4. *Playing the devil's advocate (particularly in meetings).* Assigning a person(s) whose job is to counter every argument or decision is another way to discover different options and get people communicating.

BATTLING THE STRESS THAT WORK AND CONFLICT CREATE

Few would dispute the fact that conflict produces stress, or that stress in the form of safe and regular physical exercise is good for you. However, physical exercise is voluntary and by its very nature allows the body to rest and rebuild afterward. Work-related stress is different. It grips and doesn't let go, thereby grinding the mind and body down day after day after day. Don't be someone who dies at age thirty-five but isn't buried until eighty-five. Here's how to cope with workplace stress:

- *Take control of your situation and life.* Know your limits and avoid unrealistic deadlines.
- *Pace yourself.* Try to do high-priority tasks first. Stay flexible and slow down.
- *Periodically stop and relax.* It's a mystery as to when we ever got it into our heads that work is something we can escape from each evening (historically, when has that ever happened?). So find time(s) to relax throughout the day, even if all you can muster is fifteen minutes with your eyes closed (some studies suggest that the best way to optimize this is to do so on your back on the floor).
- *Open up to others.* Discuss problems, fears, and frustrations with those you can trust.
- *Do things for others.* Selflessness is a great stress alleviator. If you want to reduce your own tensions, think about someone else's needs and satisfy them.
- *Exercise.* Engage in regular, measured, physical activity.
- *Balance work and recreation.* Schedule periods of recreation and quality time apart from work. No one can give 100 percent of his or her physical and intellectual time day after day, month after month, without some form of down time. To do otherwise

invites anguish, sickness, disability, and perhaps even death. Few people die uttering the words, "I wish I'd spent more time at the office."

- *Don't look for relaxation in the form of a bottle.* Whether through pills or alcohol, don't try to escape work pressures via chemically induced means. It doesn't work.

PUTTING IT ALL TOGETHER

The reason why the founding fathers of the United States felt so strongly about freedom of speech is because they fully understood the need for debate and dissent. Yet of all human trials and tribulations, wisely catering to differences of opinion must certainly be among the most difficult. For more ideas on how to harness conflict and make it work for you, reconsult: Chapter 4, "Understanding the Importance of Customers" (particularly the section titled "Dealing with Difficult Customers"); Chapter 6, "Getting the Most from Employees"; Chapter 7, "Organizational Structures and Cultures"; Chapter 8, "Managing Change"; Chapter 10, "Managing Teams and Work Groups"; Chapter 15, "Management: Theory versus Practice"; and Chapter 19, "Dealing with People in the Workplace."

Chapter 10

Managing Teams and Work Groups

Apart from the word *quality,* perhaps no other word in management is used and abused more frequently than *team.* In a business sense, the word **team** refers to a group of people who get together (or are forced together) to accomplish a **goal.** Using the word implies that everyone in an organization is happily working to fulfill a common purpose. The truth of the matter can be somewhat different.

For the most part, the reason for forming teams is to produce **synergy**—often explained via the mathematical equation that $2 + 2 = 5$. Put another way, the caliber of a team's work is usually expected to exceed the sum of what each individual can produce on his or her own.

A **work group** is defined as two or more individuals who get together to accomplish a task or goal. Although it may be fine to make a distinction between teams and work groups in an academic setting, in a business organization the expectations for both are the same. In any company, whether you're assigned to a team or a work group, you will be expected to perform as a unit and produce results. Common sense dictates that the wider skill and knowledge base of a group of people has a distinct advantage over that of one person. Although no one in the real world—apart from motivational speakers and consultants—believes that $2 + 2 = 5$ (or that 110 percent of anything can be achieved), the purpose of a team *is* to

- bring out the best in each member (motivate),
- help formulate ideas **(brainstorming),**
- conduct feasibility checks on ideas (reality test), and
- in general, complete a task better (or perhaps more uniquely) than can reasonably be expected of an individual.

Teams work best in environments requiring change or innovation, but the key to their performance hinges on cooperation, coordination, conflict handling, and commonality. In other words, teams work only when the basic social skills taught in kindergarten are put into practice. The problem is that many of us all too often need to relearn these basic manners. This means that time and effort is needed before teams can be relied upon to run smoothly and produce results, because the people within them will usually, at first, seek to satisfy personal ambitions.

TYPES OF TEAMS

Teams or work groups (the terms will be used interchangeably from here on) usually fall into three categories:

1. *Cross-functional teams* (also known as *committees* or *task forces*) consist of individuals who come from different departments, different schools of thought, and/or different work areas. The idea is that different mind-sets working together have a better ability to see the bigger picture. Cross-functional teams are known to work particularly well when it comes to product development as well as large, complex situations. The downside, however, is that they tend to take a great deal of time to manage and "get the ball rolling."

2. *Problem-solving teams* are designed to solve problems or give suggestions, not to implement these solutions. Historically, solving problems is the reason teams and work groups were first formed in business environments.

3. *Self-managed teams* are problem-solving teams that have the ability (and authority) to regulate themselves and enforce decisions. Studies show that self-managed teams work best when handling equipment purchases, customer problems, establishing departmental policies, scheduling jobs, and enforcing rules. Although self-managed environments can lead to an increase in work satisfaction (and has led to much positive press), the jury is still out regarding their long-term effectiveness. Absenteeism and high turnover are sometimes common with self-managed groups.

DEVELOPING A FUNCTIONAL TEAM

Teams generally develop in five stages:

1. *Forming* or selecting the people who will be on a team. During **forming** everybody is usually very polite and quiet. Group members will want to know what they will be asked to contribute and what the group will offer them. Conflict is seldom voiced and is usually suppressed. Since the grouping is new, most people are guarded and reserved in their comments and opinions and may defer to those who appear to be leaders.
2. *Storming* is characterized by personality clashes, faction forming, fights for domination, and much talk with little listening. During **storming** the group splits into separate factions and battle lines are drawn. Most important to note is that very little communication occurs at this stage. In most businesses, this battlefield scenario rarely erupts into a readily observed situation. Instead, emotion and conflict seethe beneath a veil of civility and are transformed into sarcasm and innuendo. Failure to pass through this stage without intense conflict resolution may result in lasting liabilities.
3. *Norming* begins when a team settles down and begins to work toward its goal. During **norming** the group finally recognizes that it must work together, or perhaps it's told that it must—or else. In-fighting subsides. Bickering, fighting over turf, playing politics, and, in effect, canceling each other out, reduces. **Norms** (acceptable standards of behavior) begin to be established. Most important, people start to listen to each other.
4. *Performing* develops when the group begins to work within a system that allows it to get the job done, and when everyone's input culminates into a single, shared outcome. During **performing** individuals feel free to express their views and support one another. In doing so, a clear and stable structure develops. More to the point, this is the stage during which the elevated performance of each individual emerges.
5. *Adjourning* involves reviewing results and disbanding the group. During **adjourning,** particularly with temporary or task-oriented groups, a time always comes for group members to disband and return to their former positions within the business.

Ideally, the group does so with a sense of accomplishment. Although adjourning may sound like the easiest of the five stages, it is not. In the IBM story discussed in Chapter 7, the employees who had saved the day returned from their liberating assignment only to be shoehorned back into the rigid folds of the company—and as a result (or so the story goes), each one quit within a year.

Making Groups Work

During any of the five stages of team development, problems can occur. For this reason, many groups need a *facilitator*—a person whose role is to draw the group's attention to any agreed-upon norms as well as keep them on track toward their agreed-upon goal. Bear in mind that this person does not have superiority over the rest of the group; that would diminish the reason for forming a group in the first place. Merely having *respect* for this individual is the operative issue.

In theory, groups are supposed to work toward their own norms; however, when putting a group together, most managers should establish a few ground rules beforehand, such as

- the group's purpose (posted for all to see);
- attendance expectations;
- a few behavior rules (show respect: no laughing, eye-rolling, or criticism that is focused on personality rather than the task);
- work performance expectations (the standards that will determine if members are pulling their own weight and what will be done if they are not);
- methods of agreement (or dissent);
- clarity of task(s) and responsibilities; and
- handling deadlock (for example, will lots be cast or will a coin be flipped?).

These topics must be discussed, agreed upon, and written down before a group can perform. As progress is made, all decisions should be recorded on a large display board on which they can be clearly seen and referred to. Concentrating on the positives is essential. Staying upbeat is the best way to build group morale and reinforce cooperation and participation. Indeed, it may be necessary to insist that every negative criticism be accompanied by a positive suggestion for improvement.

And Now the Bad News

Despite the proliferation of stories about the success of teams and work groups, they are not a cure-all. Just as it would be absurd to ask a group of people to do something as simple as make a cup of tea, the same applies in business. Teams usually don't work well in environments requiring simplicity, speed, strong leadership, and/or cost minimizing. Waterman and Peters (1980) cite a classic example when they discovered a large corporation that had 325 task forces, none of which had completed its specified duties in three years and none of which had been disbanded.

To add to this, strong evidence has shown that assigning people to groups can sometimes decrease their performance. **Social loafing** is defined as the tendency for some individuals to reduce their efforts when working with others. Perhaps the reasoning is that they hope to disappear into the crowd—or maybe they think that since others aren't pulling their weight they don't have to either. The result is that a few lazy individuals enjoy the hard work of others. The larger the group, the greater the chance for social loafing to occur. So what possible solutions are there to help combat this?

OVERCOMING THE OBSTACLES OF A TEAM

From time to time, every group must avoid the danger universally known as **group think.** This is best illustrated through the stereotyped "committee mentality" in which too much analysis leads to paralysis and nothing gets done. Likewise, a committee's solutions may not appeal to anyone, or be so far removed from the initial problem that they're meaningless. Group think or stagnation occurs when the smug air of superiority creeps into a team and the team refuses to consider what it feels are different or disturbing viewpoints from outsiders. As a result, contradictory data is ignored or shelved, other alternatives are not considered, and jumping to conclusions or inactivity may dominate. Group think and social loafing are best avoided by

- assigning a team member to play devil's advocate at each group meeting;
- holding second-chance meetings after a consensus has supposedly been achieved;
- not being partial to only one course of action (perhaps make it a rule to always come up with two or three alternatives);
- going "around the table" with assembled team members and insisting on **feedback** (this helps prevent quiet people's opinions from being withheld and bigmouths from dominating discussions);
- encouraging team members to do their own research and conduct their own fact-finding investigations;
- remembering that the point of formulating a group is to *produce results*—groups are not automatically a solution in themselves; and
- understanding that since every group is unique, each one will require a different start-up, functional style, and form of leadership.

Although it may be true that "many hands make light work" and "two heads are better than one," whenever two or more people work together the notion that "too many cooks spoil the broth" must be considered. In this regard, some academics make a distinction between teams and work groups—and that's fine. In the world of business, however, the concept of teamwork (the process of people working together as a unit to achieve common goals) applies to both terms. Whether you wish to call a functioning unit of employees a team or work group is up to you. The point is that in every business, employees must make a commitment to work together, serve one another, fulfill a common purpose, and hold themselves mutually accountable. Anything less and the group of employees is merely a crowd.

Chapter 11

Managing by Objectives

Of the many management fads that have surfaced over the decades, *goal-setting* is one of the hardiest. Formulated in 1968, it continues to be the basis behind many modern management techniques. Goal-setting makes three important claims:

1. Specific goals increase performance more than ambiguous goals.
2. Difficult goals, when accepted, result in a higher performance level than easy goals.
3. Providing good feedback produces more results than not saying anything.

As it so often happens in management literature, someone somewhere along the way took this proven formula, hung a few baubles on it, renamed it "management by objectives," and pretended something new had been discovered. But I digress.

As with much in management theory, the idea behind goal-setting or management by objectives is a simple one: People work better when they know *exactly* what is expected of them. Before that can happen, however, these same people need to know where they are as well as the direction they're going. With that in mind, the following three-step process should help create a starting point and bearing.

GOAL SETTING: A THREE-STEP PROCESS

Step 1: Create a Vision

In business, the word **vision** is usually so clouded in hyperbole it's misinterpreted as being synonymous with either a fantasy or predicting the future. Vision has nothing to do with a crystal ball. Rather, it's a clear and vivid idea of how things should be. When written down, a good vision is a simple yet highly motivating means of uniting people toward a common purpose and direction. This does not pertain to pie-in-the-sky dreams or financial goals ("We will reduce costs 14 percent by next quarter," or "Our aim is to increase production by 8 percent"). Instead, visions tend to move hearts and minds.

Dr. Martin Luther King Jr., one of the world's greatest speakers and humanitarians, said in his famous speecn in August, 1963, "I have a dream that my four children will one day live in a nation where they will not be judged by the color of their skin but by the content of their character." Note that he did *not* say, "I would like to see a future in which 32 percent of our nation's congressional representatives are people of color." Instead, Dr. King relayed the direction he thought his country should go in a way that most people could passionately understand—using children as an example of how things should be instead of the way they were. That's vision.

The story behind the personal home computer provides another good example. For a long time most people believed that only universities and/or government organizations had a use for computers. But Stephen Jobs (the inventor of the personal home computer) thought differently. Instead of dreaming about quarterly earnings, cost reductions, or annual percentages of growth, he envisioned computers being reduced in size, simplified, and made available to everyone. Then he did something about it. That's vision too.

Step 2: Decide on a Mission

Once a vision has been formulated, the next phase is to come up with a company **mission statement.** A mission statement individualizes a business by clearly defining its purpose and uniqueness. In doing so, mission statements usually share four common traits:

1. They set tough, but obtainable, standards.
2. They relay basic beliefs, values, and priorities.
3. They are measurable.
4. They clearly explain what business the company is in.

Mission statements can be a page or two in length or a simple, one-sentence statement proclaiming that a company will surpass its main competitor in two years. Either way, they should avoid generic blurbs. Mother and apple pie platitudes such as, "we will not just compete, but advance," "our purpose is to satisfy our customer's needs and wants," "we will provide even better service in our field," and "our mission is to be number one" look great, but are hardly inspiring. In place of these worn-out clichés, a clear, unique, and unambiguous message should be made that everyone takes seriously. An example of this comes from the Newport Shipping Company of Rhode Island: "We will build great ships. At a profit if we can. At a loss if we must. But we will build great ships."

It can be argued that this statement is as bad as the previous examples (why mention operating at a loss?), but the statement still gives me pause. In all my years in business I've never heard the mission of a business put quite this way and it leaves me with no doubt that the Newport Shipping Company places a heavy emphasis on quality, pride, and teamwork.

Years ago the Ford Motor Company came up with its own version of a marketable mission statement that was used to create improvements in many of its operations: "Quality is Job 1." Note that an emphasis wasn't placed on sales figures or cost cutting or production quotas. Instead, the mission was *quality*. Everything else was done in pursuit of this. Just as important, concentrating on this one attribute prevented the company from spreading itself too thin by trying to be all things to all people—which no organization can do.

Step 3: Breaking the Mission Down into Achievable Objectives

Objectives are blueprints for achieving a mission. They address both financial and nonfinancial issues, incorporate concepts of time and measurement, and are designed to be more concrete and action-oriented. If, for example, a company's mission includes "making our product(s) accessible to everyone in Central Europe," the company's objectives may be "to have employees focus on sales and marketing strategies," or "for our factories to eliminate waste by 6 percent," or "to provide better home delivery service to our customers."

These objectives would then be further broken down into more specific targets for unit or departmental use, perhaps with an interpretation along the lines of, "This will be achieved by getting our people excited about what we do," or "We will establish closer links with our clients." Solutions for reaching these objectives can be as diverse as implementing employees' ideas, using flexible work hours, improving working conditions, investing in new equipment, providing improved training, establishing better reward systems, or a host of other *workable* ideas. A good way to determine if objectives are viable is for administrators (the people that determine a business's vision and mission) to walk the shop floor, talk to customers, ask questions, then shut up and *listen*. Doing so will provide a firsthand account of the match between the business's capabilities and the wants and needs of its external and internal customers. In the process, the language of everyone concerned is better learned and an understanding is reached of what best motivates the organization and how hard employees can be pushed.

An Example of Aiming High but Staying Grounded

Not long ago an industrial bakery in Great Britain decided that it wanted to become the country's leading manufacturer of bread and rolls *(vision)*. The idea for achieving this was to greatly improve customer service *(mission)*. To this end, new technology and equipment was purchased and employees were trained in new procedures in order to speed up operations *(objectives)*. Yet nothing much happened. Unable to explain why, the CEO decided to go on a fact-finding mission. To his surprise he discovered that the manufacturing side of the company was creating far more bread than the packaging section could handle. The result was a bottleneck of breathtaking proportions. Flabbergasted, he pointed to an old packaging machine and asked why it wasn't being used to help prevent the bottleneck. Nobody knew. As it turned out, when a new packaging machine had been purchased the old one had been shut down. Again, no one knew why, but when it was switched on it was found to be in excellent working order—and in the course of an afternoon the bottleneck was eliminated. The CEO decided then and there to make factory visits a part of his weekly routine. This led to him growing closer to his employees, which in turn enabled them to shed their fear of asking and answering questions. That resulted in most employees spontaneously generating new ideas and trying new things (work ownership). The result? The company is now one of the United Kingdom's leading bakery product distributors.

MANAGEMENT BY OBJECTIVES

One of the basic concepts of management by objectives is the elimination of ambiguity. Only then will employees understand what the business's objectives are as well as how and when they are expected to achieve these goals. Essentially, the procedure looks similar to the following:

1. Identify, discuss, and determine the organization's goals (i.e., its vision and mission).
2. Break the organization down into units. What is it that everyone in these units is supposed to be doing in relation to the company's overall goals?
3. Together with employees, establish *specific* goals for each unit and person. This should include both quantity and quality expectations for every task. Remember, these goals must be challenging but achievable.
4. Prioritize the goals. Employees may need help placing them in the company's preferential order.
5. Clearly state a realistic deadline for goal completion. As the old saying goes, without a timeline, goals are nothing more than dreams.
6. Build in feedback mechanisms so employees know exactly how they are doing.
7. Ensure that an appropriate reward system is linked to results.

That's It?

When you stop and consider that many organizations (1) place a wall between management and nonmanagement employees, (2) don't take the time to fully train employees, (3) don't do much of anything in regard to educating employees in the company's overall goals, (4) are satisfied when employees simply maintain the status quo, and (5) provide little or no feedback during an employee's workday, the value of managing by objectives becomes more obvious.

Warning! In Management, Panaceas Don't Exist

Managing by objectives is a fundamental management concept, but it does have its drawbacks. For example, goals can sometimes be seen as a ceiling rather than a floor. In other words, once targets have been obtained, employees have been known to stop performing.

Equally, setting objectives that are too demanding can encourage people to cheat. In fact, one of the problems inherent in management by objectives is that an emphasis can be too easily placed on quantity rather than quality. But fear not. There are solutions, and they can be found in the next chapter.

Chapter 12

Quality

Quality is the elimination of variation.

W. E. Deming

It must be said again that possibly no other word in the management lexicon is as misused as quality. Most business magazines or books are absolutely brimming with stories about how implementing quality resulted in massive savings, enormous efficiency improvements, and a sea change in employee performance. Unfortunately, in almost all cases, little if anything is mentioned about how this new-found quality was acquired. Therein lies the wrinkle, because quality isn't about a cost-saving idea or a spectacular work-check program. Rather, it's an all-out, do-or-die, in-your-face, bottom-line, fanatical way of thinking. But first, a little history.

ACHIEVING QUALITY

The father of managing quality is considered to be W. Edwards Deming. During World War II Deming established spectacular results in various lines of production (upwards of 200 percent improvement) by believing in the value of employees. He stated that most troubles faced by companies begin at the top by managers who place more emphasis on numbers than people and believe that superficial gimmicks and slogans can substitute for real improvement. He also said that the common workplace, riddled with fear and shortsightedness, often resists innovation and change through counterproductive internal competition (Deming, 1986).

Deming found that employee respect, input, and involvement unleashed the kinds of improvements that met the challenges of competition and a changing marketplace head on. Unfortunately, when the war ended and the troops came home, the age-old practice of dictating from the top resumed. During this same period, Japan was desperate to recover from its losses. For decades it had suffered a terrible reputation for making cheap, low-quality goods, so when it came time to rebuild, the country decided to change this reputation. In 1951, Deming was invited to Japan to explain quality-control techniques, and as a result, the quality of many Japanese products has become legendary. Today, the highest award a Japanese company can win is the "Deming Prize"—an honor so prestigious it's awarded on national television.

W. Edwards Deming's Points for Achieving Quality

- Create a culture that regularly asks for, and accepts, innovation.
- Invest heavily in training and research.
- Spend revenues on maintaining current equipment as well as acquiring new items.
- Work to improve every system—not just the end result of that system.
- Ask for statistical evidence of processes.
- Eliminate financial goals and quotas.
- Learn to motivate rather than give orders.
- Take the fear out of the workplace by providing an environment of constant learning.
- Break down barriers between departments and place an emphasis on communication.
- Eliminate superficial goals and slogans.
- Retrain people in new skills. (Deming, 1986)

Condensing the Master

Deming's concept of quality has since been reduced to three important concepts and rechristened *total quality management:*

1. *Quality is defined as the ability to meet customer needs 100 percent of the time.* Because this is a statistical impossibility, perhaps it's best to think about it this way: Quality is an ongoing process. In every conceivable way quality is a race without a finish line because it requires a dedicated commitment to continuous improvement. Perhaps one of the loftiest goals in the quest for quality is that of *zero defects*

(managing an operation that runs perfectly; creating a product that never needs improving, and so on). As with achieving customer satisfaction 100 percent of the time, obtaining zero defects is probably unobtainable. So why bother? Once again, it's better to view zero defects as a *means* to an end rather than an end in itself. For example, the reason why we educate ourselves and read management books isn't because we seek perfection but rather improvement. Most of us know that perfection is unobtainable, yet that doesn't prevent us from going through the perfection process. So it is with quality. Again, it's the unending *process* that counts.

2. *Quality revolves around making improvements in everything an organization does.* This requires an intense focus on the customer. Keep in mind our definition of the word *customer* (everyone an organization serves) and you'll start to understand the difficulty inherent in instilling quality into a business. Simply put, quality involves breadth and depth in its implementation. If you recall, this means every department in an organization must be made aware of the need for quality (breadth) and every individual within these departments must be actively involved in the quality process (depth). The entire concept of quality therefore hinges upon a shift in perspective from management to its workforce. Too many managers think it's their duty to determine quality work solutions. The error in this line of thinking is that quality isn't just a management issue—it's everybody's issue. In the search for quality, employees have to be trained to not only seek out problems but to continuously find their solutions as well. This takes time and effort.

3. *Quality must be viewed as a measurable degree of excellence.* Quality entails looking at all of an organization's systems and then breaking them down into countable units (the number of goods produced, the number of customers served, the time it takes to perform a task or service, the costs involved in a process, the number of errors made, etc.). Only when everyone has access to an accurate system of measurement can a determination be made as to whether or not what is being measured is good, bad, or average. Against this, improvements can be judged.

MEASURING QUALITY

The Eight Dimensions of Quality

According to D. A. Garvin (1987), competing on the basis of quality requires identifying and enhancing its various dimensions. Doing so will help a business gain a competitive advantage in the marketplace. Following are Garvin's eight dimensions of quality:

1. *Aesthetics:* how a product looks, feels, sounds, tastes, and/or smells
2. *Conformance:* the degree to which a product meets established standards
3. *Durability:* the amount of use a product provides before it fails
4. *Features:* the "bells and whistles" that supplement the function of a product or service
5. *Perceived quality:* the product's reputation
6. *Performance:* a product or service's main operating characteristics (i.e., how well does it do what it's supposed to do?)
7. *Reliability:* the time period in which a product malfunctions or fails
8. *Serviceability:* the speed and courtesy of attention given to customers as well as the competence and satisfaction with which a business offers repairs (Garvin, 1987)

Benchmarking

A term frequently used in connection with measurement and quality is **benchmarking.** To put it bluntly, benchmarking involves copying (or stealing) somebody else's ideas, the process of which follows:

1. It begins with a home business using another company's program(s) or idea(s) as a reference point.
2. A study is then carried out to determine what makes this program (or company) so successful.
3. An analysis is done to find out if ideas gathered from the other company will fit into the home business.
4. The challenge at this point is to try to implement the ideas of the successful company into the home business.

For example, a local health club may discover that a competitor has a big screen television mounted in its cardiovascular room so customers can watch programs while riding exercise bikes. The local health club then does the same thing. In a similar vein, major corporations routinely copy the services, operations, billing setups, and other systems of their rivals. Even unrelated industries can generate benchmarking ideas. Stories abound about how IBM used a Las Vegas casino's security systems as a benchmark to reduce employee theft. Another story involves a Chinese clothing manufacturer using a McDonald's menu format to simplify its product offerings. A colleague told me about an airline that once reviewed an Indy 500 pit crew to see if any ideas could be implemented in its quest to speed up baggage control systems.

PUTTING QUALITY INTO ACTION

Of all the areas that quality needs to permeate, one of the most important is customer service. Simply put, basic business survival is contingent upon providing *what* customers want, *how* they want it, and *where* they want it. If it's unknown what customers want, then they need to be asked (for a reminder of this concept, please review Chapter 4). Any attempt toward quality without the input of customers is a complete and utter waste of time—and could very well set a company marching off in the wrong direction.

Since quality is both a state of mind and a task-oriented concept, it can't and won't be achieved simply through an edict issued by senior managers. For quality to be all-encompassing, it must begin at both the top and bottom of an organization. Following are two plans to get you started. Keep in mind that for either of these plans to succeed, the determination of a zealot must be maintained, the patience of Job endured, and an extraordinary amount of persistence exhibited (you may also wish to refer again to Chapter 10).

Plan A

1. Gather your employees together and highlight a simple problem of which everyone is aware. Make sure the problem is work-related and is something that can be changed.

2. Become enthusiastic about finding a solution to the problem and look for a quick way to resolve it. This should be done with everyone's input.
3. Set a target and implement the solution.
4. When the solution has been implemented, praise and reward everyone.
5. Find another problem and repeat the previous steps (perhaps asking someone else to be the initiator).

Plan B

1. Formulate a weekly *quality circle* meeting. Quality circles are comprised of anywhere between two to twelve individuals from a department whose assignment is to make improvements.
2. Create an atmosphere in which employees are unafraid to voice their opinions and comments.
3. Provide your quality team(s) with the appropriate training or educational material on problem solving, group issues, and other quality related topics.
4. Establish a few basic ground rules outlining what you want to achieve.
5. Give your team(s) time to gather confidence.
6. Keep it going.

Again, it's of paramount importance that the establishment of quality involve *every* aspect of a business. Nothing should be overlooked because *everything* an organization does is interlinked and requires constant attention, upkeep, and care. Even an issue as seemingly trivial as the cleanliness of an organization's washrooms will reflect on the standards set in work areas, and that ultimately sends a message about the amount of respect given to both internal and external customers. This concept is aptly illustrated in a nursery rhyme:

> For want of a nail, the horseshoe was lost
> For want of the shoe, the horse was lost
> For want of the horse, the rider was lost
> For want of the rider, the battle was lost
> For want of the battle, the kingdom was lost
> And all for the want of a nail.

The Mother of All Battles

Quality is more than just a term—it's a commitment to undertake unending, backbreaking work. As an ongoing crusade it's also a long-term goal, and long-term success should always be given precedence over short-term gains. To establish quality, time must be devoted to making products or services that work right the first time. Staff training and development must never be sacrificed. Reliability should always take priority over speed. For each and every employee the pursuit of quality must become an unassailable state of mind, or the kingdom will be lost.

Chapter 13

Ethics

Pick up a newspaper or turn on a television or radio and nine times out of ten there'll be a story about a company being accused of dishonesty. The tobacco industry, for example, is reeling from their decades of lies. The Enron scandals of 2002 resulted in the bankruptcy of the world's seventh largest corporation, thousands of job losses, and the demise of Arthur Andersen, one of the largest and, up to then, most prestigious accounting firms on the planet. After the terrorist attacks in the United States on September 11, 2001, several local hotels raised their rates knowing that journalists and aid organizations would be arriving en masse. A few years ago a study concluded that *all* whitening toothpastes don't whiten teeth in the manner their manufacturers claim. Every year cosmetics companies are taken to court for producing materials that don't reverse the signs of aging or reduce cellulite. Other products kill or injure their users only to have the companies that produce them deny it or cover it up. Let's also not forget the clandestine polluters, the unfair competitors, the inside traders that leave the rest of us out in the cold, the cheaters, the greed mongers, and the fat-cat CEOs who destroy company market share and are rewarded with dismissal packages worth hundreds of millions of dollars.

But all is not lost. The reason these folks are in the news is because they got caught. Although the bad things we see may be just the tip of the iceberg, people who behave unethically usually get what they deserve.

ETHICAL BEHAVIOR

Learning Right from Wrong

Ethics can be defined as the factors that make a person or business good, moral, truthful, honest, and sincere. Behaving ethically means acting with integrity, thinking of others, saying what is meant, and meaning what is said. Similar to quality, ethics is an all-encompassing concept. You can't be "a little bit" ethical or "for the most part" ethical. You either are ethical or you aren't. Can ethics be learned or taught? Some people say yes, others say no. At the very least most of us do know the difference between right and wrong. Perhaps for many people the real question behind ethics is, "will I get away with it?" These days, the answer to that question is increasingly "no."

From a management perspective, therefore, behaving ethically is an integral part of long-term career success. Since customers today have access to more information and have more choices than ever before as to where to take their business, it only makes sense to behave ethically.

Reasons to Behave Ethically

From an internal customer's (employee's) standpoint, behaving ethically

- produces a sense of pride in the workplace (and that helps motivate workers);
- sets a good example (it's difficult to demand that employees be honest if managers aren't); and
- raises an organization's level of perceived fairness.

From an external customer's standpoint, a company's ethical behavior

- decreases the chances of being sued;
- provides another good reason to buy your products; and
- raises the level of social consciousness for all involved.

FOUR LEVELS OF ORGANIZATIONAL ETHICS

When making day-to-day decisions, every business consciously chooses to what extent it wishes to be responsible to its internal and external environments. There are four basic levels:

1. *Social disregard* occurs when a company, for the most part, does whatever it wants, regardless of the consequences.
2. *Social obligation* is when a company chooses to meet its legal responsibilities and nothing more.
3. *Social responsiveness* is when a company changes its policies and practices in regard to social conditions or pressures. For example, pressure from consumer groups was so strong that several tuna manufacturers eventually decided to buy tuna from fishermen who used dolphin-friendly harvesting methods. Now, whenever shoppers see the words "dolphin friendly" on a tuna label, the businesses providing that tuna benefit by selling what the public wants.
4. *Social responsibility* occurs when a company decides to pursue long-term goals that are good for society overall. An example of this is The Body Shop, a cosmetics company founded on the basis that cosmetics should not be tested on animals. For the company's founder, reducing animal cruelty helps make the world a better place.

UNETHICAL VERSUS ETHICAL
DECISION MAKING

Rationalizing

How do otherwise intelligent people make unethical decisions? Usually by kidding themselves with the following justifications:

- *It's only a* little *unethical.* Perhaps the rationalization is that "everybody else is doing it," or the outcome seems trivial. Either way, it boils down to doing something wrong. Eventually someone will be held accountable for it—particularly if a scapegoat is

being sought or someone is seeking ammunition against someone else.

- *No one will find out.* "Unless it's discovered," goes the argument, "it's not really unethical." Baloney. Little these days goes
  undetected and very few people are bright enough to commit the
  perfect crime. It may take a while, but someone, someday, will
  probably find out what was done and by whom. If you're stupid
  enough to do something unethical, you're stupid enough to get
  caught.
- *It's in everyone's best interest.* For example, if your business
  sells its products overseas and a buyer demands that a bribe be
  paid or else another supplier will be sought, what do you do?
  This is a very difficult dilemma. Overcoming this situation depends in part on the ability to look beyond short-term gains and
  address long-term implications.
- *My company will stand behind me.* Yeah, right. And so will
  Santa Claus, the Easter Bunny, and the Tooth Fairy.

How to Make an Ethical Decision

Make no mistake, people who act unethically do so at their own
peril. Most of us do know the difference between right and wrong,
however, when the world produces its myriad shades of gray, put
yourself through both rounds of the following questions to ensure
that a good decision is being made:

Round 1

1. *Legality:* Is what you wish to do legal?
2. *Fairness:* How will the decision's outcome affect the people
   who are involved with it?
3. *Self-respect:* Do you feel good about the decision and its outcome?
4. *Long-term effects:* Shortsighted solutions are rarely an answer.
   Will your decision create or destroy job security? What are the
   risks and dangers? How will your company's internal and external environments be affected?

Round 2

1. *Purpose:* Do you understand and accept the real reasons or intentions of what is being done?
2. *Perception:* Have you considered the feelings and well-being of those affected by your decision?
3. *Persistence:* Have you remained flexible to other people's viewpoints yet committed to your own faith and beliefs?
4. *Perspective:* Did you comprehend the whole picture and determine what is really important?
5. *Pride:* Will your superiors be happy with your decision? Does your organization want to be held accountable for it?

A Good Litmus Test

If you're ever in doubt as to whether something you wish to do is unethical, ask yourself the following question: "Would I do this in front of the boss (or my spouse or partner, or my children, or my friends)?" If the answer to this question is no, you have your answer to the first.

WHISTLE-BLOWING

Much of the world's unethical business practices are brought to light by **whistle-blowers:** people who expose the dishonest and/or criminal acts of others. Ironically, in many countries, whistle-blowers are detested and called a variety of names including snitches, rats, grasses, and other derogatory comments. Personally, as a manager, I used to both love and loathe the people who brought me information I might otherwise have never known about. At one end of the scale, these people were indeed tattletales. At the other end, they provided me with many under-the-surface-problems that could be resolved before they erupted, thereby preventing future catastrophes and ultimately improving the business (as well as my reputation as a manager). For the most part, despite all the good that whistle-blowers do, they tend to be stigmatized and often face impaired career development, termination from their jobs, and/or other forms of retaliation—

even when they save lives. Following are some "dos and don'ts" for whistle-blowers.

Dos

- Make certain a full understanding of what is happening is ascertained and that any allegations are *absolutely* correct.
- Talk to an attorney to ensure your rights will be protected and that proper procedures will be followed (*you* may be in trouble otherwise).
- Keep accurate records to support your claims. Make copies and keep them in different locations (not your office).

Don'ts

- Don't assume the law protects you.
- Don't talk to the media first.
- Don't expect a big financial windfall if you end up being correct, are fired, or are retaliated against.

THE BOTTOM LINE

Being ethical doesn't cost anything. Being unethical can cost dearly. Don't be fooled into thinking that unethical actions won't be discovered. Employees aren't stupid and they do know just about everything that's going on in an organization. It may sound trite, but unethical practices make us all poorer in almost every conceivable way. No one gets ahead in life by being unethical. What goes around comes around, and the bottom line is that if you're honest and can take pride in your life, your decisions, and your business—you *will* be repaid in kind.

Chapter 14

Leadership

Great leaders write new stories.

Carlos Ghosn, President
Nissan Motor Company

Leadership is a notoriously difficult concept to grasp, but it's not due to a lack of information on the subject. Most bookshops are literally bursting with material on leadership. What makes the subject difficult to pin down is that virtually everyone has an opinion regarding what constitutes effectiveness—and ultimately, being effective is what makes a leader. Add to this the too many people out there who seem to find no shame in calling themselves leaders and the concept becomes even more difficult to define.

LEADERSHIP VERSUS MANAGEMENT

For the most part, **leading** involves motivating people as well as building commitment toward a set goal (which in any business should be serving internal and external customers). So how does leadership compare with management? **Management,** it can be said, is about coping with complexity: bringing about order, consistency, and profit by drawing up and successfully implementing plans and structures, then measuring them. **Leadership,** on the other hand, is about coping with change: establishing a vision, effectively communicating it, and inspiring others to work consistently toward it. To put it more succinctly, *things* are managed. *People* are led. In fact, one of the more important aspects of leadership is that it doesn't occur unless others are willing to follow.

According to research, business leaders generally fall into two categories: those who place an emphasis on a *concern for task* (getting a job done by strictly meeting work objectives), and those who focus on a *concern for people* (getting things done via relationships and the consideration of others). Which is the most effective? In practice, good leaders probably combine both categories—using whichever method proves most reliable in the situation encountered at the time.

LEADERSHIP: ABILITIES AND ACTIONS

Beauty is in the eye of the beholder suggests an old saying. The same can be said about leadership. Indeed, one of the greatest determinants of leadership is hindsight. For example, American presidents Abraham Lincoln and Harry S Truman are today almost universally recognized as effective leaders, yet in their time they were widely derided. Conversely, think of the business leaders in the 1990s who were once held in high regard. Only later were some discovered to be liars, incompetent, scandalously greedy, and/or out-and-out crooks. Clearly, a rush to judgment, emotion, politics, public relations (spin), and a disregard of common sense often factor heavily when awarding leadership status. The following attributes, however, are more substantive when determining the characteristics of a leader.

Abilities

The following personal traits often lay the foundation for leadership success:

- *Above-average drive:* initiative, high energy, and a strong appetite for achievement
- *Motivation:* a desire to lead and influence others
- *Integrity:* honesty in dealing with others and consistency with words and deeds
- *Self-confidence:* being naturally decisive and confident with personal abilities
- *Intelligence:* able to gather, integrate, and interpret complex information
- *Vision:* a good understanding of present situations and how the future should be

- *Flexibility:* being willing and able to adapt to changes
- *Inspiring confidence in others:* to be measured, not necessarily by how many followers a leader has, but by how many leaders he or she creates

Actions

Successful leaders often possess the following result-producing styles:

- *Excellent communication abilities:* the ability to convey clear, short, understandable messages
- *A willingness to make sacrifices and display personal risk:* seen in televangelists who constantly remind everyone that their devotion costs them dearly (usually with the example of friends who abandoned them after they found God), or a politician's "I was born in a log cabin" type story, or an executive stating that he or she came up in the business the hard way
- *Exhibition of extraordinary behavior:* standing out in a crowd and making tough decisions
- *Instigating change:* leading changes rather than the other way around
- *Showing sensitivity:* being aware of the needs and wants of others
- *A willingness to be reliable and responsible at all times:* running a company is not unlike being the captain of a ship—even when not on the bridge, a captain is still on call and responsible for whatever happens
- *Handling adversity with grace:* remaining calm, professional, and polite under pressure

COMING TO GRIPS WITH LEADERSHIP THEORY

Among the dozens of tomes that try to explain leadership (one or two actually suggest that the loss of a parent is contributory), some of the more recognized have come to the following conclusions. Note that almost all of these theories appear to have their roots firmly entrenched in the concern for task versus concern for people categories mentioned previously.

- Fiedler's (1992) Contingency Model states that good leadership depends on matching or changing appropriate leadership styles (concern for task or concern for relationships) with the proper situation or best "fit."
- The Hersey-Blanchard (1998) Situational Theory suggests that successful leaders should adjust their styles (delegatory, participatory, persuasive, or forceful) depending on how ready and willing others are prepared to follow.
- House's (1990) Path-Goal Theory says that an effective leader is one who allows people to achieve their own task-related and/or personal goals (the leader helps set goals, removes barriers, and provides rewards).
- Blake and colleagues' (1964) Leadership Grid splits leaders into a grid with axes marked "concern for people" and "concern for production." Leadership styles are then marked accordingly, with the one at the upper right-hand corner being the most effective because it represents leaders who show a very high regard for both people *and* production.
- The Vroom-Jago (1998) Leader Participation Theory is designed to help leaders choose a decision-making method for solving problems. For example, with an *authority decision,* the leader makes the decision. With a *consultative decision,* the leader consults others and then decides. And with a *group decision,* both the leader and his or her followers participate and decide.

Drucker's Three Essentials of Leadership

Over the decades one of the more down to earth management writers has been Peter Drucker. The following list is Drucker's explanation of what constitutes leadership:

1. *Defining, communicating, and establishing a sense of mission in a way that's understandable to others.* This means establishing an organization's direction, priorities, and standards, and simply and effectively stating them. Put differently, a leader is someone who, in the midst of chaos, is "the trumpet that sounds a clear note."
2. *Treating leadership as a* responsibility *rather than a rank.* Good leaders accept their weaknesses and surround themselves with talented people. Doing so means they're not afraid to develop

strong and capable subordinates and they don't blame others when things go wrong. Although effective leaders do not normally treat all people similarly, they don't appear unfair when doing so.

3. *Earning and maintaining the trust of others.* Effective leaders display above-average levels of integrity despite evidence that suggests they sometimes lack in morals. For example, U.S. President Bill Clinton produced eight years of unprecedented growth and prosperity during his two terms in office, but severely tarnished his reputation after lying about a sex scandal and putting his country through needless embarrassment. His successor, George W. Bush, moved into the White House after a questionable election, decided to fight terrorism after initially ignoring it, created the largest debts in history, invaded Iraq while misleading the public, repeatedly changed his justifications for the Iraq invasion to suit current events, and pointlessly drove a wedge between America and its allies. Despite their faults, however, both men maintain devout—almost rabid—followers. Go figure.

The conclusion? Few, if any, leadership discourses mention winning-at-all-costs, arrogance, or ruthlessness as measures of leadership. Rather, in a statement that suggests most organizations are overmanaged, under led, and too public-relations oriented, Drucker suggests that effective leadership isn't based on being clever or deceiving; it's based on being ethical and consistent in word and deed.

THE NATURE OF LEADERSHIP

Leadership, Hype, and the Human Element

It's been said that the great leaders have great weaknesses. This means that leaders are all too human and that their strengths and weaknesses must be carefully considered to determine if and how they will best suit a business's needs. The successful manager of one company may prove disastrous as head of another.

For example, the founder of Chevrolet, Louis Chevrolet, left his firm after a heated disagreement with a financier. Later he beat Anton

Champion (of the spark plug company that bears his name) so badly Champion had to be hospitalized. Yet the Chevrolet company is still going strong, so fists-a-flying Louis must have done something right. That being said, would his tactics work elsewhere? Would you want to work for him?

Legendary manager Soichiro Honda, apart from reportedly liking a drink or two (or three) had a reputation for losing his temper with shoddy workmanship and hitting the responsible employees over the head with whatever tool was available. Yet he was also renowned for allowing workers to speak their minds and for listening to what they said.

Jack Welch, the former CEO of General Electric (GE), was proclaimed by many authorities to be the most successful manager of the last quarter century (1975-2000). However, when he retired in 2001, GE's stock price plummeted. In addition, the company's spectacular annual growth rates, which Welch regularly crowed about, fell under intense questioning because, according to some, they had been exaggerated and couldn't be proven. GE's accounting and risk management sections have since been accused of all kinds of business and accounting "shenanigans" (*The Economist*, 2002, p. 63). Welch was later further disgraced when upon divorcing his third wife it was revealed that he had wrangled a retirement package worth hundreds of millions of dollars (he has since rescinded the deal) that would have allowed him to be treated like a king, at GE's expense, for the rest of his life. If there's a lesson to be learned from all of this it must surely be that if you encourage an image of perfection, you'd better be perfect.

Last, consider Winston Churchill. Although a highly competent man, Churchill was notorious for making big mistakes that cost lives (the Gallipoli massacre being just one). He was also renowned for being sour and cruel to his subordinates and had a remarkable propensity to burst into tears. Despite this reputation, however, he was one of the few people in his day who understood that winning a war involves fighting and suffering losses. Ironically, just about everyone who put up with his surliness loved him (probably because he instilled in those around him a sense of genuine purpose). Nevertheless, immediately after he led the saving of the free world, British voters threw him out of office. Not because they disliked him but because they felt he wasn't sensitive enough to their needs after so many sacrifices had been made.

It cannot be overstated that the negative and positive aspects (the human elements) of an individual should be examined against a company's strengths, weaknesses, culture, and character before he or she is tapped to undertake a leadership position—and this must be done while keeping in mind that no one is, or ever will be, perfect.

Are You a Leader? A Practical Example and Exercise

Curiously, some people think that because they've been promoted to, or find themselves in, a leadership position, it automatically makes them a great leader.

Here is an exercise I give my students. It never fails to make an impact.

A few years ago, a female physician (Dr. Jerri Nielsen) volunteered to be the medical officer for a research facility in the Antarctic. The facility is situated in an extremely remote area that accommodates only a dozen or so scientists at a time. Because of the extreme cold (which has been deemed "searing") there are only a few weeks out of the year when a plane can land, pick up or unload passengers, and deliver supplies. At all other times aircraft fuel becomes gelatinous because of the cold. In other words, once someone commits to this project, they're stuck there for a full year.

Shortly after winter set in Dr. Nielsen discovered that she had a virulent form of breast cancer. Taking into account her surrounding resources she sat down with her colleagues and discussed the tasks each would have to perform in order for her to survive. One person would have to operate (incredibly, Dr. Nielsen remained awake during the surgery and told this person what to do *while it was being done*). Another person who knew how to work with chemicals had to learn to administer chemotherapy. Still others came up with a means to transmit pictures of blood and tissue samples to outside medical experts via a jury-rigged digital camera, a mobile phone, and a satellite hookup.

Thankfully, the story has a happy ending. Dr. Nielsen survived her ordeal and was eventually airlifted out of the Antarctic in a heroic rescue attempt weeks later. Needless to say, she learned many important lessons along the way.

When relaying this story, I ask my students to place the following list of people in the order of their importance to an Antarctic research station:

> Manager (the person responsible for instilling teamwork, cooperation, and purpose)
> Doctor (the person entrusted with saving lives)
> Researcher (the person who checks facts and gathers information)
> Chemist (the person who understands how chemicals and elements work)
> Scientist (the person who conducts experiments and gathers data)
> Mechanic (the person who fixes equipment)

For many by-the-book managers the logical answer would be to assume that everyone is equally important. But as we've seen before, management can be a contradictory subject.

So who is at the top of your list? The doctor? The manager? How about the bottom of your list? Did you select the researcher or the mechanic?

From her experiences, Dr. Nielsen identified the mechanic as perhaps the most important person in the group. Why? In the Antarctic, a good leader knows that the environment is the greatest enemy. Although each person in a scientific team is fully expected to pull his or her own weight, if something were to happen to the electrical generators or if the heating system shut down *everyone* would be dead in less than forty-eight hours unless a mechanic was available to fix the problem.

Dr. Nielsen went on to explain in her book, *Icebound: A Doctor's Incredible Battle for Survival at the South Pole,* that she also came to appreciate the sometimes conflicting interrelation between type A personalities (bold, aggressive, decision-making types), who turned into caged tigers during the Antarctic's dark months, as well as the importance of the quiet, type B personalities who exhibit patience, silence, and pragmatism. Once again, a good business leader fully understands concern for task versus concern for people situations and applies his or her leadership qualities accordingly to ethically achieve appropriate objectives and overcome adversity.

So, After All Is Said and Done, What Exactly Is Leadership?

Being named as the head of an organization does not automatically make someone a leader. Leading consists of convincing others to go places they have never gone, do things they have never done, and accept situations they have never encountered. Accomplishing this usually involves Handy's six methods of influence (described in Chapter 5) combined with the abilities and actions mentioned earlier in this chapter. With such a heady mix of conflicting traits and styles, not to mention the polarizing interpretations of followers, it's no wonder the subject continues to baffle so many. Perhaps leadership is best summed up with the famous words uttered years ago by a United States Supreme Court Justice (or Senator or a famous movie mogul, depending on who you believe said it first) when weighing a subject he was having difficulty grasping. "I may not know how to define it," he said, "but I know it when I see it."

Chapter 15

Management: Theory versus Practice

When I was a toddler, my mother used to place me in a playpen with my brother while she cleaned the house. One day, after she'd done this for the hundredth time, she heard me crying and rushed back to see what was wrong. To her surprise I was covered with bite marks—deep, angry, red-and-purple welts that sprouted over every inch of my body, including my face. She glared at my angelic-looking brother who quietly pretended that nothing was wrong. "Bad boy," she said, wagging her finger at him, "bad boy!"

Unfortunately, my brother decided he was onto a good thing. As time passed, whenever no one was looking, he continued to bite me. Not knowing quite what to do, my mother asked her local doctor for advice. "Maybe if I just bite him back it'll teach him a lesson and he'll stop," she said.

"No," replied the doctor, "don't do that. It'll cause more harm than good. Just be patient, continue to reprimand him, and he'll soon get tired of it."

But of course he didn't. Mom next sought the counsel of her friends.

"Maybe I should just bite him back," she pleaded.

"Oh, God no! You should never bite your child," replied one friend.

"Why not keep just them separated?" asked another.

Mom buried her face in her hands. She had had three boys in one year (yes, you read that correctly) and it was impossible to keep us separate. We simply had to learn to sit together peacefully. Although all the material on children who bite relayed calm, rational solutions, not to mention reams of explanatory theories, each was adamant about one thing: "Whatever the urge," they warned, "don't ever give in to the temptation of biting your child back."

Some time later, after watching my brother sitting silently beside me without any outward sign of mischief, she left the room, confident that the biting phase of childhood had finally passed him by. In less than a minute the sound of me crying filled the house. Infuriated, she stormed into the room, strode over to the playpen, grabbed my brother's arm, and bit him.

"And it wasn't just any old bite," she told me years later. "I bit him hard."

"Didn't he cry?" I asked, unfazed. My mother was a formidable woman in her day.

She reared her head back in amusement. "Oh my, yes! He was so loud I thought the windows would crack!" She leaned forward with a glint in her eyes. "But he *never* bit you again."

What does this story have to do with management? Read on.

In 1960, a man named Douglas McGregor published a book titled *The Human Side of Enterprise*. This was not just any book. *The Human Side of Enterprise* became one of the most important books on management ever published. In fact, some experts believe it's the most influential book on management that's ever been written. In it, McGregor formulated his X and Y theory of human nature. This theory states that people can be classified into two categories. The X category presents an essentially negative view of people. It suggests that individuals regularly avoid responsibility, dislike work, have little ambition, and need constant supervision. The Y classification takes the opposite approach. It assumes that people enjoy responsibility, like to work almost as much as they like to play, and when given the chance will exercise good judgment and self-direction. McGregor's conclusion is that Theory Y best captures the true nature of employees, and managers should practice the appropriate methods to take advantage of this type of behavior. In practice, McGregor's management motto can perhaps best be summed up as "softly, softly."

Unfortunately, the real world crept in. Make no mistake, McGregor was a very intelligent man (he taught at the Massachusetts Institute of Technology [MIT], which has been rated as the number one school in the United States for many years). Sometime after coming up with his theory he was offered the job of president of Antioch College. Naturally, he jumped at the chance to put his theories into practice, but after six years at Antioch, bravely admitting that his philosophy and management skills had failed, he resigned and returned to teaching at MIT. In his farewell address at Antioch, McGregor unabashedly explained that being a manager involved being authoritative—that meant enforcing policies, punishing slackers, playing politics, and facing responsibilities and difficult decisions with grit and resolve. Management was not, as he had thought and despite all his research, merely an advisory function.

To his credit, when McGregor returned to MIT he continued to advocate the Theory Y approach to management despite his own failings with it (i.e., he recognized that the fault lay with the messenger, not the message).

The point of these two stories is that the key to good management lies in maintaining a balance. Few if any management books seem to acknowledge that managing people is not always sunshine and sweetness (the words "hard work" are about as far as most authors go). When all is said and done, good management means having the backbone to use the stick approach when carrots cease to work. That's not to say this book advocates using unpleasantness as a management tool. Constant anger, threats, tantrums, and other dramatics in the workplace are self-defeating and usually nothing more than signs of insecurity. Yet when all other methods have failed, a little sterner stuff used within the boundaries of fairness and prudence sometimes goes a long way. Maybe a thousand years from now, when humanity has progressed to an age in which reason and a quiet word are enough to alter behavior, the anger and/or a raised voice in the workplace will become unnecessary. Until that happens, however, keep in mind that most employees are made of fairly resilient stuff. When they decide to test your resolve, which they inevitably will, your only option, after all else has failed, may be to bite back.

A PRACTICAL EXAMPLE

In 1994, a business I was managing acquired a new software system I'd ordered to improve customer service. Most of the company's employees were quite eager to learn this new system and several of them often stayed on in the evening past their shifts in order to become adept at its intricacies. One woman, however, held back. Realizing that fear was probably behind her excuses, I arranged for one of the staff to privately tutor her in the afternoons, but to no avail. She always insisted she had too much work to do. I then signed her up, at company expense, for a computer course located about a block from our offices. She never attended a single class. By then it became clear that no amount of persuasion was going to work. She'd simply decided that she wasn't going to use the new software program and she had quietly dug in her heels. Shortly thereafter I called her into my office, pointed out the different alternatives that had been provided to her, and issued an ultimatum. Her job required that she learn the new system, I explained. Everyone else had to gain these new skills (including myself) and she could not be the exception. In the meantime, the company had lost time and money because of her procrastination, not to mention her successful defiance of my authority in full view of everyone. "You have a choice," I said, "either you learn to use the new system within three weeks or you'll be fired."

Ironically, three weeks later, she was the employee that sang the praises of the new system the loudest. As I'd hoped, it had lightened everyone's workload considerably.

THEORY VERSUS PRACTICE: A METAPHOR

An adage states that "everything looks good on paper." Management theory is no exception. It almost always looks and sounds great—until it's applied. I'll use skiing to illustrate this point. Studying skiers, talking about skiing, watching ski films, reading books and articles, and conducting interviews is all very well and good, and necessary, when trying to understand the concept of skiing. Yet, until you strap on a pair of skis and set off down a snow-covered hill, fully appreciating the combined elements that constitute successful skiing will prove elusive. The next time you want to put theory into practice, replace the following skiing terms with the name of the theory and act accordingly.

- Skis are necessary for skiing. They are not wholly suitable for other purposes.
- Skis can be dangerous to those who do not know how to use them and even those who do. Avoid danger by regularly updating your knowledge as to how they work.

- Using skis properly and without malice provides consistent and immediate feedback. Learning to interpret that feedback is not a sign of failure—it leads to future success.
- Skis aren't designed to humiliate people, hold grudges, or accept excuses.
- Skis treat people equally; they do not play favorites.
- Skis are immune to power plays, whims, and emotions.
- If you're not using skis, you're not skiing—and you're not a skier.

For additional ideas on the subject of putting theory into practice as well as motivating and disciplining employees, please refer to Chapter 6, "Getting the Most from Employees"; Chapter 19, "Dealing with People in the Workplace"; and Chapter 28, "Tools for Developing External and Internal Employees."

Chapter 16

Managing in Different Cultures

There's much more to working in a foreign place than reading, memorizing, and conforming to stereotypes. Indeed, the quaint practices mentioned in many books have long since vanished in much of today's business world, especially when it comes to other countries. Examples include these:

> Don't show the soles of your feet in the Middle East.
> Don't touch the head of someone from Asia.
> Burping after a meal in some countries is a way of showing satisfaction.
> Don't talk business over lunch with the Spanish or Germans.

To make a long story short, if you're in doubt about how to behave in another nation or with a person from a different culture, do a bit of genuine research first. Some common sense wouldn't hurt either. Perhaps people from Asia don't like having their heads touched, but would you do this in a business setting in *any* country?

One Middle East business for which I had the pleasure of working contained more than fifty-two nationalities all under one roof (described at length in *Fundamentals of Leisure Business Success,* The Haworth Press, 1998). Since it's impossible to know the intricacies of fifty-two nationalities, most employees simply made the effort to be polite with everybody at work and that was all that was needed. Of course, that was at *work*. Many nonnationals, including quite a few Muslims, found it increasingly difficult to *live* day after day in a strict Islamic culture. In fact, throughout my tenure the number of individuals I met who sold their homes, left their jobs, and uprooted their families to move halfway around the world to a land they never bothered to investigate was astonishing. Incredibly, eleven individuals (and their families) were in my original orientation group, but after nine months only four of us remained. I shudder to think of the money, time, and energy this regularly costs both the company and the people who quit.

CULTURE AND HUMAN BEHAVIOR

What Is Culture?

Culture is a *learned* way of life that predominates a nation, society, or group. These learned behaviors include the following:

- Social organization (including class systems, caste systems, and social welfare or the lack of it)
- Religion (the inseparability of religion and government versus the secular approaches of the West)
- Customs, holidays, and rituals
- Values, attitudes, and education
- Political and legal systems (the last time I was in Singapore, for example, behavior as benign as chewing gum was against the law)
- Language
- Music, arts, and literature (conservative and liberal views are very different in different places)
- Work practices (for example, some cultures make it a rule to meet with several people at once rather than give one person a prearranged time of undivided attention)

Trying to Understand Human Behavior in Different Cultures

Generally speaking, we all tend to have similar wants: hope, a safe place to live and work, a future for our children, respect, and so on. What makes us different, as groups, is the way we attempt to achieve these wants. When we see others achieving their wants differently we usually cast a judgment. This can be explained via the **attribution theory.** In part, the attribution theory states that most people believe behavior is either *internally* caused (under the personal control of the individual) or *externally* caused (resulting from outside influences). A conclusion is dependent on three factors:

1. *Distinctiveness:* Is the behavior unusual?
2. *Consistency:* How often is the behavior displayed?
3. *Consensus:* Does everybody display the same trait?

Unfortunately, most of us have a built-in bias called the **fundamental attribution error.** This is based on the all-too-common belief that other people's behavior is almost always internally based rather than externally based. We'll readily believe that an employee's poor performance is due to laziness rather than faults with management or the company, or that the reason why someone appears aloof is because he or she is rude when it is instead due to a death in the family. Always judging others on an internal basis is tantamount to the joke about the English-speaking person who visits a non–English-speaking country and loudly laments that everyone there speaks a foreign language.

ERRORS IN CULTURAL PERCEPTIONS

Shortcuts in Judging Others

Whether internal or external, perceiving and determining why others do things differently is often a burden. As a result we tend to take shortcuts called **selective perception.** Sometimes these shortcuts can be valuable, but more often than not—particularly overseas—they can cause trouble. This is because humans generally react to their *perceptions* rather than to *reality.* Following are a few common misplaced perceptions:

- *Assumed similarity:* Assuming that other people are just like us and therefore go about their business the same way we do (all people are as ambitious, hardworking, have the same fears and concerns, and are as interested in something as we are).
- *Stereotyping:* Forming a general opinion based on a number of perceptions (real or otherwise) that we have of a particular group.
- *Halo effect:* Making a general impression based on one character trait. For example, we see or meet a man from an unfamiliar

place and assume that all people from that culture are just like him.

Emotions and Culture

Emotions are intense feelings directed at someone or something. Generally speaking, there are two types of recognized emotions:

1. *Felt emotions:* An individual's *actual* emotions.
2. *Displayed emotions:* Emotions that are expected or considered appropriate. In other words, displayed emotions, like cultural traits, are *learned.*

Felt and displayed emotions are often different in other cultures. When people working overseas for the first time begin to deal with employees and customers they sometimes naively assume that the emotions they're encountering are emotions these people actually feel. But again, that is a *perception.* Not long ago, a group of Americans was asked to match pictorial facial expressions with six basic emotions, and 86 to 97 percent of them agreed on the results. However when faced with the same pictures, the Japanese obtained only a 27 to 79 percent agreement. The point is that displayed emotions, like cultural differences, are *learned.* For example, in the United States it's considered normal for service-level employees to act overly cheerful and friendly with customers. However, in Israel this is sometimes interpreted as a sign of unprofessionalism. In Saudi Arabia it can be seen as a come-on that could land you in a lot of trouble.

CULTURE SHOCK

The Reality of Living Closely with a Different Culture

Culture shock is defined as the confusion, disorientation, and emotional upheaval that follows a move (not a visit) from one country to another. Every person that moves to another area of the world inevitably suffers through the following four stages, although most people deny that it ever happens to them.

Stage I: Excitement, pride, enthusiasm, and novelty character-ize this stage. Being selected to represent your company in an international location is usually an attribute to your abilities and talents, and it's only natural to feel on top of the world during the first few weeks or months of the new job.

Stage II: Reality sets in. Factors such as not being able to speak the local language, which at first seemed somewhat humor-ous, now becomes a struggle. Menus, schedules, billboards, even radio and television programs are unintelligible. Simple conversation becomes a chore. In essence, everything you do requires much more effort than previously imagined and there seems to be no escape. (This can last two to three *long* months.)

Stage III: The struggle to adapt to a different language, foods, work patterns, schedules, customs, and so on turns into despair, depression, anger, or perhaps even defiance. Some people never quite get out of this stage. Symptoms include yearning for your place of origin, bad-mouthing everything, and gener-ally being miserable. Turning to alcohol or any number of other self-destructive behaviors is not unusual for those who can't, or don't want to, cope during this period of adjustment.

Stage IV: The learning and acceptance process begins. At this stage the newcomer begins to understand what is and isn't important in the new culture and stops battling against all the differences being encountered. Instead, he or she learns to concentrate on maximizing the opportunities available in the new culture rather than focusing on what is different and/or unavailable.

Interestingly, once an individual leaves his or her adopted country and goes back home, this entire process is repeated—albeit much more quickly.

Smoothing the Transition

Here's how to smooth a move to another culture before leaving:

- *If possible, develop personal friendships.* This can be a slow and arduous process, and it isn't always realistic, but it can provide you with a good head start.

- *Conduct continuous research.* Undertake research for both general background information and basic business knowledge.
- *If possible, visit the country, region, or organization to which you plan to move.* This is invaluable for developing firsthand experience.
- *Talk to some born-and-bred locals.* People from the country you're moving to can be invaluable in teaching you the acceptable procedures. More often than not, when it comes to learning about their country, they'll be happy to help.
- *Use local distributors and agents.* National bureaucracy and distribution systems can be a nightmare. Again, since local people have a better understanding and familiarity of the marketplace, try to use them whenever possible.
- *Develop language skills.* Language is an essential part of a country's culture. Although mastering another language may not be feasible, attempting to learn as much as possible will impress others—and your initiative *will* be rewarded.
- *Use common sense.* Basic etiquette, common courtesy, speaking quietly, and showing respect will lessen most cross-cultural faux pas.

COMMUNICATING IN DIFFERENT CULTURES

Effective communication is difficult under the best of circumstances. However, four specific problem areas have been identified in relation to cross-cultural communication:

1. *Semantic barriers.* Words can have different meanings to different people. For example, the words *meeting, bizarre,* and *rendezvous* are more formal or are more powerful than most non-English speakers are aware.
2. *Word-connotation barriers.* Similarly, words can imply different meanings. In Japanese, the word *hai* translates as "yes," but it means that a person is listening, not that he or she agrees.
3. *Formality barriers.* In some cultures, language is changed when used in a formal sense rather than an informal one. Know the limits and correct uses of addressing others before you open your mouth.

4. *Perception barriers.* Different cultures view the world in different ways. For example, in some countries overpoliteness is sometimes seen as rude while in others too much casualness can be seen as lacking in manners. Again, familiarize yourself with local customs *before* you make a mistake.

The following tips will help minimize cultural misperceptions and misinterpretations:

- *Assume differences until similarity is proved.* You are far less likely to make an error if you assume that others are different rather than assuming they're similar.
- *Study what is said rather than your interpretation of it.* Interpretations are usually culturally sensitive. Delay making judgments until sufficient time has passed to think about what was said.
- *Empathize.* Before communicating, put yourself in the recipient's shoes.
- *Be careful with your conclusions.* When you think you've understood something, treat it as a hypothesis first. Be ready to modify your conclusion as time passes.

Being a Welcome Guest: The Art of Listening

Many people confuse hearing with listening, but the two are not similar. *Active listening* requires a listener to fully understand an intended message. Here's how it works:

1. Make eye contact and offer affirmative head nods and other appropriate expressions.
2. Listen for *message content*. What exactly is being said?
3. Ask questions, but don't interrogate. As the saying goes, "if you want to be interesting, be interested."
4. Try to understand the speaker's feelings.
5. Let the speaker know that his or her feelings are important.
6. Note any nonverbal cues. What does the speaker's body language suggest? Are any mixed messages evident?
7. Paraphrase and restate. Repeat to the speaker what you think you're hearing. Statistics state that 60 percent of American and

European companies identified poor or insufficient feedback as a primary cause of bad employee performance.

8. Don't overtalk.

IN CONCLUSION

Living in another country (or even another region of your own country) requires much restraint, hard work, and understanding, but it's also incredibly rewarding. My international experiences, both good and bad, have made my life immeasurably more interesting, humbled me, tested me beyond belief, and made me and my work more marketable. In addition, living abroad has broadened my mind and even changed a few of my political views, but the opportunities that have unfolded (and continue to unfold) have been breathtaking. Although I now feel comfortable just about anywhere, being surrounded by different cultures (which is an integral part of my work) is still an uphill climb. I still make mistakes, use the wrong words, and assume what I shouldn't—I just don't do it as often. It may sound corny, but poet Robert Frost was right when he said "I took the [road] less traveled by, and that has made all the difference." If you ever get the chance to work abroad and the offer is both legitimate and compatible with your personality and ambitions, go for it. Remember that good and bad are found every place you go—just as at home. After arriving in a new culture, let the air out of your ego, stop insisting that (and acting like) your culture is superior, lower your voice, concentrate on the good, avoid the bad, and don't compare everything to that tiny, closed-minded comfort zone you've created back home (I promise you that the fantasyland your nostalgia creates doesn't exist). Only then will you be well on the road to enriching yourself in ways you never thought possible.

PART III:
THE BASIC SKILLS OF MANAGEMENT

Chapter 17

Managerial Decision Making and Problem Solving

Making decisions, both large and small, is a large part of a manager's daily life. In graduate school one of my finance teachers (a formidable man mentioned in this book's preface) started one of his lectures by proclaiming "If a good manager has ten decisions to make, he or she will probably get four right, two wrong, and the rest, well, it really doesn't matter."

It took me awhile to come to grips with that statement. What he meant was that not all decisions are necessarily right or wrong. In many instances, it is the *degree* to which they are right or wrong—as well as how an organization chooses to *deal* with its decision—that is just as important as the decision itself. A spectacular finish can be achieved after a bad start. It's up to each business to determine whether its decisions become successes or failures (i.e., the only true mistakes made in life are those allowed to continue as mistakes). Take a look at two examples:

The Tylenol poisoning crisis. In the 1980s a murderer opened a package of Tylenol pain capsules, poured out the contents of several, and replaced the ingredients with poison. Several people died as a result. Instead of distancing itself from its responsibility, the makers of Tylenol decided to inform the world about what had happened, ordered all its medications pulled from store shelves, assisted the FBI in its investigations, and made an effort to solve any future problems by developing tamper-proof packaging. As a result, the problem quickly disappeared. Shortly thereafter the company was widely praised for its response and it resumed business having earned an enormous amount of public respect.

The Firestone tire debacle. In the 1990s, reports accumulated suggesting that the tires Firestone made for sport utility vehicles (SUVs) had an inherent fault. Firestone publicly announced that it didn't really need to look into the situation. Instead, the company blamed the SUVs as the culprit. Of course, the SUV manufacturers blamed Firestone. Meanwhile, deaths from accidents resulting from tire blowouts continued to rise. In the end, as sales plummeted, the situation brought Firestone to the brink of ruin and several executives lost their jobs.

MAKING UP YOUR MIND

Several books claim that there's a big difference between managerial **decision making** (the process of finding and making a choice among alternative courses of action) and **problem solving** (the process of identifying and resolving the difference between what is actually happening and what should be happening). Any further elaborations will end here. Yes, problem solving and decision making are unique processes, but most decisions are made (or problems solved) in one of three ways:

1. *By avoiding the decision or problem:* ignoring the warning signs, doing nothing, and hoping the problem goes away (as Firestone did)
2. *By battling the problem:* taking action on problems as they arise (as Tylenol did)
3. *By preventing problems before they occur:* proactively finding ways to deal with future problems (as Tylenol also did with its innovative new packaging)

Two styles tend to be employed most when making decisions or solving problems. The first is called a *systematic approach.* This involves tackling problems in a rational and analytical fashion. It usually translates into breaking a problem down into small components and addressing each one in a logical manner. The second style is referred to as the *intuitive approach,* which allows for more flexibility and spontaneity. With the intuitive approach, experience and creativity are key.

Which style is the most effective? That depends upon the person involved in the decision making as well as the circumstances. Obviously it might be risky for an inexperienced manager to rely solely on gut feelings to make a decision. On the other hand, analyzing the minutiae of every decision option can be time consuming and tedious. In reality, most managers boil these processes down with a judgment call. So perhaps the overall question is: How good is your judgment?

GOOD PROBLEM SOLVING AND DECISION MAKING:
A STEP-BY-STEP APPROACH

Several years ago I was appointed the general manager of a number of recreation facilities scattered across an area comprising more than two million people. One day early in my tenure a call came in from a cleaner at one of the swimming areas. A teenage boy had broken in and been caught swinging and jumping on a large canvas structure designed to provide shade. As a result, the structure had collapsed.

This was my wake-up call that vandalism was a rampant problem. Searching through the files later, it became apparent that my predecessors had done little to solve the problem. "These things just happen," was the attitude most of the staff had taken. Since we were located in the middle of a desert I cringed at the number of complaints we would receive because the shaded area was no longer available to our customers. In addition, the business was woefully short of cash, so our options were limited. I asked the cleaner to get the boy's correct name and address and send him on his way.

Sometime later, after visiting the scene, I telephoned the boy's parents with the hope of seeking reimbursement. By then the teen had been able to concoct a well-rehearsed lie. Imagine my surprise when I was informed that I had physically abused him (I hadn't come within miles of him) and his parents were considering taking legal action. Fed up with the attitude of "not-my-child" parents, I presented myself to the company's director. As I hoped, we began preparing for war.

To make a long story short, we let the matter drop. Simply put, doing nothing is sometimes the right decision. In every situation there comes a point when the effort and expense behind the process far outweighs possible conclusions. Besides, it rapidly dawned on me that I was ultimately to blame for the situation. Here's why, along with the steps that were taken to correct the problem:

1. *Every problem has a cause and every situation an alternative.* Find it. Investigate, dig deep, and get as many opinions as possible. Asking why five times is an old yet still an effective way of getting to the heart of the issue.

   Regarding the boy who pulled down the shaded structure I had to ask myself (and the staff) many questions and confront a series of highly unpleasant answers, among them:
   - Was the area supervised or unsupervised at the time? (unsupervised)
   - How did the vandal get into the pool area? (the gate lock was broken)
   - Had this happened before? (yes, but no one had bothered to report it)
   - How long was the lock broken? (possibly weeks, but again no one bothered to report it)

2. *Don't go it alone.* Gather as many creative solutions as you can. Get as many people involved in the decision-making process as possible (perhaps even external customers). Most important, be certain that the *cause* is being treated, not the symptom.

   The staff and I then came up with a number of possible solutions including:
   - Increase supervision of all pool areas before and after hours. If staff shortages make this impossible, assign a patrol.
   - Install "dud" security cameras (real cameras were too expensive).
   - Install/fix more sturdy locks on all pool gates.
   - Design more programs for teens (people rarely destroy what they are an active part of).

3. *Think ahead.* Whenever possible, choose the best long-term solution. Short-term solutions rarely solve anything and by definition must to be addressed over and over again.

   We then discussed the wider picture (the implications of our possible solutions) as well as putting the head of maintenance in charge of all the cleaners (it was his proposal). The idea was to train the cleaning staff to immediately report problems to the maintenance department before the facilities opened, thus ensuring that problems such as broken locks would not go unfixed or go unreported or get lost in the system.

4. *Take action.* Follow through with the decision. Often the difference between effective and ineffective managers is that effective managers are people of action.

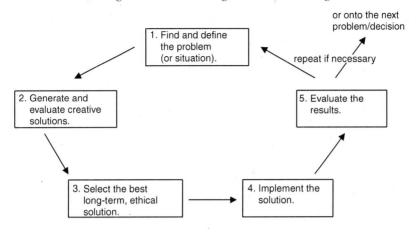

FIGURE 17.1. The Problem-Solving/Decision-Making Process

We decided to follow through with all the options we'd discussed (except installing the dud security cameras).

5. *Reevaluate the results of the decision.* Were the results effective? If not, repeat the process (see Figure 17.1).

Our actions didn't resolve every future problem, but they did reduce the number significantly (as compared to earlier years), so we decided to maintain them.

PRACTICES TO AVOID WHEN MAKING DECISIONS

Everybody at some point must make a decision. The trick is to ensure that your decisions do as little damage as possible. The following practices typically result in bad decisions. Becoming aware of and avoiding them will improve the chances that a bad decision won't happen.

- *Escalating commitment* is the tendency to increase effort and apply more resources (people, materials, money, etc.) when the chosen solution is not working. This usually occurs when people can't admit that they're wrong.

- *Heuristics* are judgmental shortcuts in decision making often based on bias, stereotypes, misinformation, gossip, rumors, outdated thinking, or other unreasonable sources and experiences. For example, choosing not to buy products in red packaging because you don't like the color red or refusing to buy products with French words in their name, even if they're American owned and operated, because the French didn't want to invade Iraq in 2003 (don't laugh; it happened).
- *Rushing* through any problem or decision-making process is a recipe for disaster. Every manager suffers through days that present a seemingly endless barrage of problems and decisions that have to be made. Don't be tempted to race through them or choose the easy way out.
- *Not putting your customers first* is a rampant managerial mistake. The world's media is full of stories about managers who put self-interests before those of their customers. The classic example happened in the 1970s when Ford created an automobile called the Pinto. Somewhere along the line it became apparent that the Pinto had a tendency to burst into flames during collisions, thereby badly burning or killing its occupants. Instead of solving the problem, the company's executives made the astonishing decision to do nothing. Their conclusion was that the amount of damages they would have to pay as a result of court actions would actually be less than fixing the car's inherent design flaw. So people continued to die and, as is the case with most bad decisions, this one came back to haunt them. *Every* decision a manager makes must be geared toward customers. Anything else is just plain stupid.
- *Relying too much on statistics or mathematical formulas* is a bad idea. Collecting and analyzing data certainly has its place, but too many people seem to forget that the world doesn't always operate with mathematical precision. More to the point, management is more of a human endeavor (i.e., dealing with common sense) than a mathematical one. A specific example of this involves a famous vacuum cleaner manufacturer in Britain. The company decided to run an offer that included free plane tickets from London to New York (and back) with every purchase of their product—despite that the price of their product was virtually insignificant compared to the cost of the airline

tickets. "But," stated the marketing department, "statistics show that customers rarely take up such offers." Thinking that it would then be a good publicity exercise, the company decided to go ahead with the plan. Needless to say, they quickly became besieged with consumers who just wanted to get at the tickets. The company immediately withdrew its offer, but by then the die was cast. They were taken to court and they lost—the judge ruling that they had to provide the airline tickets just as their offer had promised. Sometime later the company went bankrupt and was bought out by its rival.

In 2003 the president of Red Lobster was fired after approving the promotion of an all-you-can-eat crab legs offer in the United States. Unfortunately, crab legs are very expensive and Red Lobster underestimated just how much Americans could eat. The result? Contrary to statistical evidence, Americans showed up in droves—costing the company millions.

- *Reinventing the wheel* is not a logical goal. Few managerial decisions are novel. Chances are that someone somewhere has had to make a decision similar to the one your organization is facing. Before making a wrong decision or inducing an ulcer trying to make the correct one, do a little research and find out what other people or companies did when they were faced with similar situations. It may save time, effort, money, embarrassment (when someone else points out that company X did it better) and a few sleepless nights.

CREATIVITY AND DECISION MAKING

"If you think that the solution to every problem is a hammer," goes the old saying, "then you'll probably see every problem as a nail." When it comes to finding an optimal resolution to a problem, most managers tend to (1) be too conservative and miss out on a full opportunity, (2) try the same old approach they've been using for years, or (3) happily settle for a *satisfactory* solution. To facilitate an *optimal* solution when making a decision, consider the following tips from *A Kick in the Seat of the Pants* by author Roger Von Oech (1986):

- *Believe in your creativity.* If you have the right attitude and think you can be innovative and creative, chances are that you will be.
- *Encourage nonconformity.* Allow differences to be presented.
- *Reach out beyond your specialization.* Use other people to expand upon ideas and assumptions.
- *Avoid too much logic.* Don't accept the way things have always been. Ask "why?" as often as possible.
- *Search for more than one right answer.* Don't get stuck in a closed-minded attitude.
- *Step back.* Take time to think, tinker, and play around with ideas.
- *Don't be afraid of trial and error.* Accept the fact that failure is often a path to success.

A FINAL THOUGHT

We're all continually faced with the need to choose—a process often subject to distortion and bias. Unfortunately, decision making is usually based on judgments rather than a planned, logical process. Concentrating on being proactive instead of reactive is a big step in reducing problems, but the next time you find yourself face to face with a big business decision, take a deep breath, think, and get others involved. You should also apply "Round 1" and "Round 2" of the questions posed in Chapter 13 on ethics. Doing so may bring you closer than you ever thought possible to an optimal solution.

Chapter 18

Managing Time

Time is a unique and precious resource. Once lost, it can never be replaced. Although the term *time saving* is frequently used, it's a misnomer. Time cannot be saved. It's either used or wasted. In the same vein, many people make the mistake of placing time in a category similar to money. Controlling time isn't controlling finances. Yes, two minutes or two hours can be "spent" on something, but whereas monetary units rarely vary (one dollar is the same as another dollar), two hours are never the same because different things always happen in different hours. For example, certain activities may be done at one hour but not another, or people may or may not be available during different hours.

Naturally, since time is valuable, it must be managed effectively. Not doing so often results in an organization characterized by high dramas, such as the following:

1. Lurching from one task or project to another
2. Last-minute rushes to meet deadlines
3. Days and/or hours that slip by with little or nothing to show for them
4. A general degradation of performance
5. A build-up of unnecessary stress
6. An environment in which everyone runs around constantly fighting fires

The good news is that time, like any resource, *can* be managed.

UNDERSTANDING EFFECTIVE
TIME MANAGEMENT

The trick with most learned traits is to get into the habit of them—and the nice thing about habits is that the good ones are just as hard to break as the bad ones. Consider these five points:

1. *Time is allocated to everyone in equal measure.* Money, materials, and labor can be (and sometimes are) distributed unequally, but everyone has twenty-four hours in a day. With time management, the idea is to use those twenty-four hours the best way possible.
2. *Poor time management is often a symptom of overconfidence.* As with any management process, time must be planned, monitored, and reviewed. Once this is understood and *accepted,* a system can be devised to make the most of it.
3. *Work expands to fill the amount of time available (Parkinson's Law).* Put another way, if you're given an hour to perform a task that takes thirty minutes, you'll probably use the full hour. Likewise, if the task normally takes an hour and fifteen minutes, you may be able to squeeze it into an hour if that's all the time available.
4. *The most effective managers produce 80 percent of their results using 20 percent of their time.* Therefore, managers who use their time well often ensure that their most important responsibilities are included in that 20 percent of time. Everyone has a natural cycle. Some people work best in the morning, some in the afternoon. Use this cycle to its best advantage. Tackle the most demanding duties during your peak times and the routine tasks (answering e-mails, performing follow-ups, scheduling, etc.) at the slow points. Granted, this may be difficult if others have control over your time allocations, but do keep it in mind.
5. There is a major *distinction between action and accomplishment.* Being busy doesn't mean that something is being accomplished. Management involves focusing on results—not putting on a show.

Classifying Time

Two major types of time are found in most work environments:

1. *Response time:* The uncontrollable amount of time required to perform a task. For example, if a manager must attend a weekly meeting and that meeting typically lasts two hours, then that time can't be used for anything else.
2. *Discretionary time:* The amount of time that *is* under a manager's control. Sadly for many people at the low level of the management scale it doesn't amount to much, and what is available often occurs in blocks of five or ten minutes rather than hours. The trick is to learn to coordinate discretionary time so that it can be bundled into bigger and more useful units. Again, for the bottom-level manager this may be difficult—but don't despair. The suggestions in this chapter may prove helpful.

TIPS FOR MAXIMIZING YOUR TIME

Ranking Priorities

Learn to take control of your work before it takes control of you. Taking the time to think about and write a schedule may seem time-consuming and in itself a waste of time, but adopting this habit helps by

- planning each day (or week) efficiently;
- better allocating an appropriate amount of time for duties;
- eliminating the wasted time by providing time limits (remember Parkinson's Law);
- pointing out (and giving ammunition to refuse) excessive work-loads;
- monitoring accomplishments; and
- being on time for appointments and meetings.

A good way to begin time management is to prioritize or rank work activities from the most important to the least important. Every work-day contains many tasks that must be accomplished. Some are more important than others and some are more urgent. Taking ten or fifteen minutes to separate these tasks (the urgent from the important) and prioritize them will provide a good rough draft for the day ahead. Here's how to get started:

1. Make a list of your daily or weekly duties by ranking them in order of importance (those involving paying customers should come first).
2. Next to each duty write down the best or only time to perform it (e.g., some duties can be done only in the morning, others only in the evening, or on a Tuesday, etc.).
3. Determine how much time is *realistically* needed to accomplish each task.
4. Section your workday into units of time using a schedule notebook or desk diary.
5. Use the diary to fill in your *response times* first. Remember, response times are duties or obligations that can't be done at any other time.
6. Pencil in your most important or urgent tasks during the times that suit them best.
7. Last, fill in the rest of your available time slots as you go down your list of priorities. Be flexible. Nothing should be written in stone.

Avoid Classic Time Wasters

When making a schedule, two common managerial time wasters should be examined:

1. *Time spent between tasks:* Consider grouping together similar tasks to avoid having to start up each one independently.
2. *Time spent on personal or social matters:* Personal telephone calls, lengthy office conversations, playing solitaire on the office computer, and other unproductive activities have no place in a work environment. A good way to highlight this is to break down a salary into hourly increments. For example, $42,000 a year comes out to $875 a week or roughly $22 per hour. Would this amount of waste be tolerated if it involved other resources? Are all hours in a workday worth paying out $22? They should be.

Learn to Say No

One of the trickier aspects of time management involves understanding that everybody's time is valuable. Bottom-level employees may find this particularly difficult to communicate to superiors. A diplomatic way out of this predicament without being demoted or agreeing to take on more work is to show senior-level managers a copy of a typical work schedule to prove that time is indeed being used to its maximum. Otherwise, be firm but fair when you do the following:

- *Ask for clear goals and objectives.* Not long ago I was asked by the president of a small European college to set up a department based on a series of lectures I gave about entering foreign markets. His idea was to start a program that helped national businesses expand overseas. Yet when I asked him for a list of written objectives stating what he hoped to achieve he looked at me and said, "That's up to you. It'll be the first part of your job." So I turned him down. Why? Vague or ill-defined objectives waste time. When confronted with any task it's imperative that clarifications be made: What *exactly* is expected? What time limitations are involved? What resources are available? Such issues simply must be resolved before time is wasted on false assumptions.
- *Don't do the work of others.* Good employees know their responsibilities. Although it's important for people to chip in and cover shortfalls from time to time, constantly doing others' work shouldn't become a habit. This is not to say that an organization's staff shouldn't be enthusiastic and helpful to one another. Just keep in mind that help and enthusiasm don't add more hours to the day. For example, a manager shouldn't have to check a secretary's work for misspellings. The secretary shouldn't be required to cover the boss's forgotten duties. No one should have to mop up other people's messes.
- *Delegate.* Managers who refuse to delegate are likely to be frustrated people. It's simply not necessary for a manager to do everything, nor does it display good management skills by doing so. Good managers should regularly assign routine tasks to others. The bottom line: If an employee can do a job, let the employee perform it. In the process the manager may be surprised at how many "managerial tasks" are best suited to others.
- *Make appointments.* Throughout every workday a manager is beset by a host of people demanding chunks of time. One solution is to get these people in the habit of making appointments.

Although this is not necessary for every inquiry, the point is to ensure that time is being respected. Equally as important, when the appointee's time is up, politely say so.

- *Do the little things now.* Twenty seconds spent jotting down an idea or request will help you later avoid wasting fifteen minutes trying to remember it and/or wasting someone else's time reminding you. Filing an important paper now may help you avoid spending ten minutes looking for it later. Phoning or contacting a person whose input is needed during an impromptu meeting rather than putting it off for later (and finding out that your plans need to be altered) usually avoids wasting hours of time. The moral of the story? Don't let little things pile up into a big mountain of time consumption.

THE END GAME: MAKING LIFE EASIER

Of course using time effectively isn't the answer to every problem, but it can reveal or eliminate a lot of managerial ills. One of the many positive side effects is the amount of stress it reduces. For many managers, thinking about all that must be done in a day (or week) is enough to unleash an unhealthy dose of anxiety. During one of my managerial positions I used to awaken at three or four o'clock in the morning with my brain racing into gear, focusing on everything that had to be done that day. For the next several hours I'd try to figure out how on earth everything could be accomplished. However, when I began using the desk diary that had previously sat unopened on the corner of my desk (it took a lot of discipline to make using it a regular habit), it became clear what had to be done by Wednesday, what couldn't be done on Friday, what was best done on Tuesday morning, and so forth. After this became apparent, that sinking feeling that all managers experience at one time or another began to evaporate. An unexpected bonus arose in discovering that not only was there enough time to do everything, but some left over to pursue other endeavors as well.

Chapter 19

Dealing with People
in the Workplace

"My job might just be tolerable if it didn't involve people," a colleague of mine once confessed. To say the least, he was having a bad day. One of his employees had phoned in sick and his staff had spent the entire morning scrambling to cover her absence—knowing full well that she was suffering from nothing more than a hangover. That wasn't all. "Ever since the boss's wife had her baby," he continued, "he snaps and shouts at everyone because he's not getting enough sleep. Add to that the fact that our secretary's divorce has decreased her work output by at least 80 percent and it's a wonder we're getting anything done." He shook his head. Dark smudges rimmed his eyes. "People," he sighed, "who needs them?"

Well, the fact is we all need them, because, like it or not, work won't get done without them. The problem is that people invariably suffer through the ups and downs of life, and as a manager you must learn to deal with it. Some of these problems are beyond your control, some will test your character (would you fire an employee who has taken too much time off to attend to a sick child?), and some require the unpleasantness of discipline. Add to this the adage that for every negative comment leveled against an employee it takes three positive ones to negate it, and the process of dealing with people in the workplace can seem as if it were a minefield. This chapter is designed to help lead you around that minefield by getting you to think about creating a work environment that helps prevent *people problems* before they occur. It is not a definitive lesson in human psychology.

UNDERSTANDING EMPLOYEE BEHAVIOR
(FOUR THEORIES)

Maslow's Hierarchy of Needs

In 1974, the *Academy of Management Journal* conducted a survey that sought to determine the most influential theories in management. Second place was awarded to Abraham Maslow and his "Hierarchy of Needs" pyramid (1943) (Matteson, 1974). (The first place winner is mentioned in Chapter 15.) Through his famous work, Maslow stipulated that people's needs can be classified into five different categories, as listed in Figure 19.1.

Maslow's theory is based on two underlying principles: (1) everyone starts at the bottom and attempts to move up the pyramid when they see that the need immediately above is not being fulfilled, and (2) a need cannot be activated until the one immediately below it has been met.

As with many groundbreaking ideas, Maslow's theory continues to be the subject of attack. For this chapter's purpose, however, it's

FIGURE 19.1. Maslow's Hierarchy of Needs

not important whether you agree or disagree with it. The point is that all people have basic needs and they seek to fill those needs. Smart managers, when searching for ways to keep their staff motivated and content, will find out what those needs are.

McClelland's Three Essential Human Motivation Needs

Later in that same decade, David McClelland more or less continued in the same vein by identifying three needs essential to human motivation:

1. *The need for achievement:* the desire to do better, solve problems, and master complexity
2. *The need for power:* the desire to control other people and influence their behavior
3. *The need for affiliation:* the desire to have friendly relations with people (McClelland, 1961)

McClelland argued that people, over time, acquire or develop different stages of these needs as a result of their experiences. Equally, each stage involves a distinct set of work environments. It is therefore a manager's duty to recognize the needs of employees and create appropriate work settings to satisfy them. For example, delegating to others can satisfy their need for achievement or power, and the creation of quality circles and/or the setting up of project teams may help to satisfy affiliation needs.

Herzberg's Two-Factor Theory

In 1967 Frederick Herzberg devised a two-factor theory based on a broad study of people at work. Herzberg concluded that there are two categories that directly relate to job satisfaction:

1. *Work content:* what people do while at work
2. *Work setting:* the actual environment in which work is done

Herzberg stated that these two areas must be handled separately. Work-content factors involve satisfying employees' sense of achievement, responsibility, and personal growth. Work-setting factors (or hygiene factors) deal with employees' work environment. Therefore, if productivity is down and improvements must be made, a manager needs to find out whether work content or work setting needs attention. Adding piped-in music and cleaning work areas may be fine for improving employee work settings but would be useless if the problem lies with work content. Likewise, improving job titles, handing out awards, and other intrinsic factors may not help much with environmental work concerns.

Alderfer's Existence-Related-Growth Theory

Later, in 1992, Clayton Alderfer sought to improve on Maslow's hierarchical pyramid by condensing its five categories into three:

1. *Existence needs:* the desire for physiological and material well-being
2. *Relatedness needs:* the desire to improve interpersonal relationships
3. *Growth needs:* the desire to pursue personal growth and fulfillment

Alderfer's existence-related-growth theory is meant to be more flexible than Maslow's. Alderfer says that people can move up and down his hierarchy of needs at any given time. If, for example, a higher need can't be fulfilled, a lower, previously satisfied need can then be reactivated in its place in what he calls *a frustration-regression* principle.

CORRECTIVE COMMUNICATION

Regardless of which human behavior theory you subscribe to, its application begins with effective measurement and communication. "If it can't be measured it can't be managed," a student once told me. She went on to confidently conclude that this statement, or variations of it, could be used to control almost anything pertaining to management. I agree. Prompt, precise measurement, placed in the context of **corrective communication** (i.e., guidelines, objectives, and results), is arguably one of the quickest ways to avoid or handle people problems.

Corrective communication (or feedback) can be provided at three stages of a work task:

1. Before the task begins
2. During the task
3. After the task

Use of corrective communication is contingent upon the situation and motivational factors of the people involved. However, whether formal or informal, it must remain timely (the fresher it is, the better), honest, simple, and constructive. It should also avoid personal comments as well as situations that are out of the recipient's control. The following sections give examples of different types of corrective measures that exist in most workplaces.

Establishing Norms

Acceptable perimeters of behavior are set by both management and employees and can be formally written down in a "codes of conduct" format or set in a more informal fashion. Once these norms have been established, organizational culture and peer pressure rather than managerial policing enforces corrective behavior. Norms are powerful shapers of human behavior and can work wonders, but if left completely on their own they can result in bullying or chaos.

Success and Failure System

Most managers at some point set employee targets and goals. If they're too high, they may result in failure with the subsequent eroding of future motivation. If they're too easy, a sense of accomplishment will be eluded. Ideally, goals should be lofty and be set in achievable stages. Progress (or a lack thereof) can then be verified and rewarded (or corrected) at each stage by

- highlighting something positive,
- pointing out what needs improving (without criticizing), and
- suggesting how an improvement can be made.

Recognition

Employees need to feel appreciated. If an employee does something well and he or she is recognized, then similar successful behavior can be expected in the future. If no recognition takes place, then a message is sent that no one cares. Bear in mind that recognition doesn't necessarily have to be award ceremonies or cash bonuses (although these can be appropriate). Sometimes a simple word of acknowledgment is all that's needed.

Evaluations

Regular **evaluations** are a necessary way to remind employees that the work they do is being monitored. However, yearly or biannual reviews should not become a tedious and banal formality during which little or no communication occurs. Employees and managers need to know how they are doing and the effect they are having on one another. In this regard, evaluations should be a constructive exercise that clears the air and lets all concerned know where they stand, what improvements need to be made, and where they are heading. For more on employee evaluations, consult Chapter 28.

BEHAVIOR MODIFICATION

On the face of it, Newton's third law of motion, which states that every action brings about an equal and opposite reaction, applies quite readily to humans. The beginning of this chapter relays the example of an employee who dishonestly phoned in sick to work. This is demonstrated via a simple model of human behavior:

$$\text{trigger} \rightarrow \text{action} \rightarrow \text{payoff}$$

The hungover employee may have been celebrating a holiday, blowing off steam, or suffering from a personal problem (trigger). The result is that she drank too much (action) and got a day off from work (payoff). How can a manager break this cycle and prevent it from happening again? One way is through a rather draconian-sounding process called **behavior modification,** explained in the following five steps:

1. *Recognize the behavior.* Find out who or what is influenced by the employee's behavior and whether the behavior is in fact worth correcting.
2. *Analyze the behavior.* Every action is preceded by a trigger and followed by a payoff. When analyzing behavior, dig deep and find the trigger. What is the resulting action? What is the payoff?
3. *Seek possible solutions.* Calmly sit down with the person(s) involved with, or influenced by, the behavior and get some feedback. Perhaps he or she wasn't aware of the problem. Mentioning the problem may be all that's necessary for it to end.
4. *Implement a solution.* People usually don't do something unless there is a payoff. In a calm and rational manner, modify the trigger or payoff by adding a consequence that is either positive or negative (ideally, it should be positive).
5. *Monitor the results.* If the results work, continue along the same lines and look for another solvable problem. If the results fail, go back and try something else.

Perhaps the hungover employee was drinking because it was her birthday. Therefore, her behavior may be singular (it happens rarely) or normal in that all employees do this on their birthday. It could be possible that the employee had a personal problem and sought solace in a few too many drinks. In that case, perhaps she needs some time off from work to sort out her problem. A few days off now may prevent weeks of additional problems later. Either way, a good response would be to sit down with her and calmly discuss the consequences of her actions (provide her with corrective feedback). She may not be aware of the difficulties she caused and may feel ashamed and embarrassed when she discovers that everyone had to perform extra duties to cover her absence. Peer pressure or group norms may then prevent future problems. Perhaps making her perform extra duties as compensation or docking her wages as a punishment will eliminate any future perceived payoff. The behavior selected to deal with the problem depends on the employee, the environment, the situation, and the manager.

SUMMING UP

Every workforce has unique needs, every behavior instigates a unique reaction, and every problem has a unique solution. When dealing with people in the workplace, time is of the essence because customers won't wait while an organization sorts out its people problems. Perhaps this is a good time to reconsider the problem prevention attributes inherent in the four employee behavior theories mentioned earlier in this chapter. In other words, keeping a workforce content, motivated, and moving in the right direction is contingent upon dealing with people problems *before* they occur.

Chapter 20

Oral Communication
in the Workplace

Communication is about sending, receiving, and understanding information and meaning. The key words in this definition are *receiving* and *understanding.* Communication, particularly when it involves customers, is not just about transferring information from company to customer. That one-way street amounts to little more than advertising—and the problem with advertising is that there's so much of it in our lives that most people have learned, consciously or otherwise, to filter out what they think they don't want to see or hear. Therefore, if what's being conveyed isn't received properly, communication isn't taking place. Just as important, if what is said or written *has* been heard or seen yet *isn't understood,* communication still isn't taking place.

Two types of communication concern managers:

1. *Effective communication:* when the intended message of the sender and the interpreted meaning of the receiver are the same.
2. *Efficient communication:* when effective communication happens at a minimal cost to an organization. For this reason, managers sometimes e-mail messages or notices to employees instead of speaking with them (one of the more useful aspects of e-mail is that it allows a message to be delivered to hundreds of recipients as easily as it is to one).

DEALING WITH DIFFICULTIES AS THEY ARISE

Problems with communication usually involve human beings crossing wires, misunderstanding each other, or tuning out altogether. Welcome to the *problem zone* (see Figure 20.1)—an area filled with barriers and distractions, intentional and otherwise, that interfere with effective communication. Sometimes the problem zone is beyond the control of a manager, but for the most part the distractions within it can be greatly reduced with a little forethought.

The Problem Zone

Physical Distractions

Loud noises, telephone interruptions, drop-in visitors, lack of privacy, a dramatic workplace, etc., all contribute to distraction. Having the sender and recipient move to a quieter environment with specific instructions not to be disturbed can minimize many of these distractions.

Absence of Feedback

Letters, e-mails, memos, posted notices, reports, and voice messages are all examples of one-way communication. Dictatorial managers and large group gatherings in which feedback is unwelcome can also produce one-way communication. For managers, a solution could be to actively seek feedback from group representatives, or in the case of written material, ask recipients to initial it, comment, and send it back.

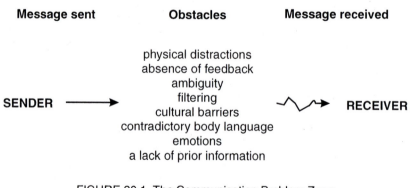

Message sent	**Obstacles**	**Message received**
	physical distractions	
	absence of feedback	
	ambiguity	
SENDER ⟶	filtering	RECEIVER
	cultural barriers	
	contradictory body language	
	emotions	
	a lack of prior information	

FIGURE 20.1. The Communication Problem Zone

Ambiguity

Ambiguity occurs when a message is unclear. This can be either unintentional or intentional. Unintentional ambiguity is often a result of misunderstanding and can arise due to a lack of leadership, too many people giving instructions, not thinking beforehand about the message being delivered, or the overuse of highbrow wording (I once overheard two department heads discuss "interfacing" with another employee—whatever that meant). However, ambiguity occurs sometimes on purpose. By being ambiguous, a manager (similar to a politician) can avoid questions and conflict, hide insecurities, make it easy to deny earlier statements, say several things at once, say no without actually uttering the word "no" and, in general, be all things to all people. The way to avoid sending an ambiguous message is to think carefully before sending it and to request confirmation of it immediately after it's been received by the recipient. The best method to avoid receiving an ambiguity is to ask the speaker for clarification.

Filtering

The intentional distorting of information to appease a recipient is known as filtering. In business this usually involves telling the boss what he or she wants to hear. Filtering has been described as one of the greatest enemies managers face. Whether the reasoning behind it is an unwillingness to identify personal mistakes, a desire to please, or a fear of retribution for delivering bad news, the results are the same. This includes making bad decisions based on distorted information as well as creating an environment that covers up errors. Wholehearted adoption of ethical policies as well as efforts toward eliminating fear from the workplace is essential for success.

Body Language

Body language is exhibited through facial expressions, eye contact, hand movements, posture, and sometimes voice intonation. Most listeners will watch a speaker's body movements (consciously or subconsciously) to discover if the movements coincide with what is being said. If not, confusion or mixed messages may result. Although this may sound trivial, inappropriate body language can unintentionally send signals of deception, dishonesty, mistrust, a lack of respect, or arrogance. Again, pay careful attention to *what* is being said and *how* it is being said. Asking for feedback is a good idea too.

Cultural Barriers

Cultural barriers exist mostly (but not exclusively) in international environments. This includes the disorientation that results from accents and/or words and actions that seem similar from region to region but aren't. For example, smiling, saying yes, and nodding when listening to a person from another culture may mean that either you agree with the subject or that you're merely listening. The best way to get around cultural barriers is to be attentive, let the other person talk freely, utilize the basic rules of etiquette, and politely ask a few questions. (Please reexamine Chapter 16.)

Emotions

Although losing self-control or displaying anger may feel good initially, it serves no purpose in the long run and is often counterproductive. Make it a rule never to address people when under emotional duress.

Lack of Prior Information

Missing information can result in a message's receiver being lost, confused, or sent off in the wrong direction. This usually happens when the sender assumes that a recipient fully understands (or doesn't need to know) the reasoning behind a message. The best way to avoid this is to remember the adage "if you assume anything, you will be wrong" before explaining something to someone.

A FEW COMMUNICATION BASICS

Years ago, when I was earning a teaching certification, an entire afternoon was spent learning to ask questions that elicited a response from students other than "yes" or "no." For those of us taking the course, this was more difficult than it sounded. Typical first attempts were similar to the following:

US: Do you understand?
THE STUDENTS: Yes.
US: Are you enjoying the class?
THE STUDENTS: Yes.
US: Is there anything you'd like us to repeat or discuss further?
THE STUDENTS: No.

The main reason we weren't getting any feedback was because of the questions we asked. Other reasons include never having shown a previous interest in the students wants and needs and therefore not yet having a trusting relationship with them. Simply put, effective communication can't start in a vacuum. It must first be *cultivated* by winning the attention and trust of the recipient. Once this has been established, asking questions that begin with the words *why, when, how, where,* and *what* will produce a greater chance of in-depth response. Try answering "yes" or "no" to them.

Silence As a Communication Instigator

Take a moment to consider using silence as a means of eliciting communication. People often become so preoccupied trying to answer someone or cut in on another's thoughts that they don't give silence a try. Most of us are usually wary of silence and try to fill it. Therefore, a way to use silence to advantage is to ask an open question (or an opinion), lean back, adopt an unthreatening posture, and await a response. The longer you remain quiet, the more detail the person will probably surrender just to fill the quiet.

A FINAL TIP

For more help developing your communication skills, as well as advice on how to establish a trusting bond with others, obtain a copy of the excellent book *How to Win Friends and Influence People* by Dale Carnegie. Don't be misled by the title. This timeless classic, first published in the 1930s and still widely available today, packs a potent message and offers a plethora of useful business advice dealing with communication, social intercourse, and their relationship in the workplace.

Chapter 21

Written Business Communication

Take a moment to study the following examples:

Example 1: In Australia, a successful businessman turns around a bankrupt company. When later asked how he accomplished this, he replies, "I forbid the writing of memos. Instead, I demanded that employees actually talk to one another."

Example 2: In Brazil, the chairman of the groundbreaking and successful company Semco describes in a best-selling book how he turned his company (and his life) around. Among the major contributing factors, he says, is the limitation of all company memos to one page in length.

Example 3: In the United States, a renowned novelist sits down to write a note to his daughter's teacher explaining the child's absence due to a medical appointment. After more than twenty minutes and numerous rough drafts, his frustrated wife finally grabs the pen from his hand and writes the note herself. It takes her less than fifteen seconds.

Example 4: Around the world, many couples forgo the option of marriage and simply live together instead. "It (the act of getting married) is just a piece of paper," many of them claim. In reply, most married people can only shake their heads, not at the act of living together, but at the absurdity of the statement.

Example 5: In the Middle East, a company manager sends out a memo to various department heads informing them of an upcoming event. Before the memo can wind its way around the organization, the event comes and goes.

Each one of these stories is true. When you get to the end of this chapter, try to ascertain the message behind each of them. For now, it's enough to know that writing is an essential managerial skill.

Among its purposes is the transfer of meaning and information from one person to another. Note, however, that differences exist between business writing and other forms of writing. Novels and stories, for example, are designed to enrich and entertain. In education, the emphasis is on imparting knowledge. With business, the point is to convey pertinent information via succinct, explanatory text.

Love it or loathe it, every manager must write competently, because the ability to write briefly, succinctly, and with clarity is considered a basic managerial strength. In fact, some estimates claim that up to 40 percent of a manager's time is spent writing.

THE ROLES OF BUSINESS WRITING

For the most part, writing in business fulfills four major roles:

1. *It conveys information.* Written words are used to communicate policies, rules, objectives, opinions, and ideas. Documentation provides a means to explain ongoing developments and plans for the future. In addition, the written word can be filed and reused as a form of definitive recording.
2. *It clarifies information.* If information or ideas aren't conveyed properly communication won't take place. Ironically, writing tends to eliminate this problem because of its complexity. No other action demands at the same time the use of the eyes (for registering what is being written), the ears (all people "hear" in their minds what they are writing as they write it), the brain (writing demands a high standard of perfection), and the hands (for the actual physical writing process). Writing forces a person to think about and plan what is being written as opposed to hiding behind the stammers, pauses, "umms," and "uhs" pervasive in verbal communication.
3. *It reflects seriousness on the part of the writer.* Some years ago I was asked to write an article for a business journal about pricing. "The first thing that must be done," I wrote, "is to get together with your colleagues and write down your business's objectives." Strangely, the journal's editors cut that sentence out—as well as the next sentence, which explained that taking the time and effort to write things down not only shows seriousness in the desire to deal with objectives but also provides a

guide that can be shared, compared, and used to measure thoughts with others (and against the future).

4. *It holds people accountable.* Poor communication is often blamed for problems or failures as diverse as (1) credibility issues concerning people who insist they were not involved with, or privy to, illegal or unethical behavior; (2) incompetence; and (3) value differences (differences in beliefs). In many of these situations initial problems may have been avoided if the use of clear, concise information was understood, agreed upon, and signed by all parties.

FORMS OF BUSINESS WRITING

E-mail

Two of the most obvious advantages of e-mail are that it's easy and it's cheap. These, however, are also its downside. With e-mail, it's easy to send hundreds of messages at the push of a button—thereby burdening employees who have to take the time to determine which messages are relevant. In this regard, e-mail has a tendency to be overused by people who don't want to communicate face to face (studies have shown that most office workers spend upward of two hours per day writing, reading, or sorting through e-mails). The cardinal rule behind e-mail (or any written business communication for that matter), apart from being considerate, is to refrain from being rude, aggressive, and/or unpleasant. Attempts at humor should also be avoided. The bottom line is that you shouldn't send an e-mail unless you can say what you've written in front of the boss. Remember, the written word, particularly on a computer screen, can be easily stored and used against you.

Memos

Internal communications designed to convey policy changes, company news, etc., can be effective in stating what actions need to be taken regarding certain issues. Generally speaking, the following format is often used as a heading:

To: (the recipient's name and job title)

Through: (the names and job titles of the individuals standing between you and the recipient in the company's chain of command)

From: (the sender's name and job title)

Date:

Subject: (a short statement describing *exactly* what the memo is about. For example, INSECTS FOUND IN OUR STRAW-BERRY ICE CREAM PRODUCTS rather than INSECTS or ICE CREAM)

The golden rule behind memos is to keep their use to a minimum. Use them only when a written record is needed. Otherwise, they become an easy way to avoid people. Also be aware that many people use memos to cover their backsides (i.e., they're used as proof that information about something was given—making those who didn't heed it look bad).

Letters

Letters are more formal than e-mails, therefore extra precaution should be taken regarding spelling, grammar, layout, and style. All letters should state the name, title, and address of the writer, as well as the recipient, at the top of the page. Letters should begin with a proper salutation and date and conclude formally with a signature. After that, the basic rules of e-mailing apply.

Reports

Reports are little more than lengthy memos. However, because reports are research based (their purpose is usually to uncover information, solve a particular problem, or present solutions), they tend to contain headings and subheadings, the procedures and/or methods used to gather information, conclusions, and recommendations. Reports often take a long time to produce because the information they require must be analyzed and compiled. This doesn't mean they must be lengthy and take a long time to read. Keep reports short and to the point.

TIPS FOR BUSINESS WRITING

Regardless of what you're writing, most objectives can be accomplished with these simple steps:

1. *Determine the aim or focus.* Have a specific *and specified* reason why your document is being written:
   - What is the intention of the document? What is it supposed to accomplish?
   - What information is necessary in achieving that aim?
   - Can you summarize its aim in one sentence and then use that sentence as the main point?
2. *Know your customer.* Convey the message in a way that the recipient(s) will understand:
   - Exactly who will be reading the document?
   - What are their likes and dislikes?
   - Is the correct tone or attitude being used to address them?
   - How much do they already know about the topic?
   - Will they understand the terms and language used?
3. *Structure carefully.* Be organized and clear:
   - Does the document proceed in a logical and organized way?
   - Does every sentence and paragraph justify itself? (i.e., is it organized around a central theme?)
   - Have enough graphs, details, and/or explanations been included to support its main point?
   - Is everything that's been written necessary? (if not, remove it)
   - Is it clear to the reader what he or she needs to know or do?
4. *Revise.* Develop and edit the document:
   - Is the document's layout effective? (are its titles, spacing, and text well-balanced?)
   - Is the document's information and style easily accessible?
   - Has someone proofread the document?
   - Does the beginning statement have a resounding impact?

More Helpful Advice (and Reminders)

- Don't try to impress others with fancy jargon or overly technical wording. For example, a friend once told me about a résumé he'd been sent that included among the candidate's former jobs "Surface Textile Application Technician," otherwise known as a painter.

- Keep everything short and to the point. Avoid long sentences and long paragraphs.
- Don't be ambiguous. Ambiguity does not reduce opposition, hide your insecurity, cut down on questions, or allow you to be all things to all people. It just makes you look bad.
- Always be certain that a written format is your best option.

IN CONCLUSION

Remember the examples presented at the beginning of the chapter? Take a moment to review them and establish a moral for each one. Do your conclusions match the following?

Example 1: Don't let memo writing or e-mails become a barrier to interpersonal communications. There is a time and place for writing in business. Learn when and where that is. Few methods of communication win out over the give and take of face-to-face discussion.

Example 2: Time is a valuable commodity for every employee. Don't waste your employee's time (or yours) with lengthy written communications that take hours to prepare and read. In most businesses, more importance should be placed on *doing* things rather than writing about them.

Example 3: A clear and precise message is of utmost importance in all written communications, but in business, unless you're a best-selling novelist with a reputation to uphold, Pulitzer prize-winning prose isn't necessary. Trying to achieve literary merit in a business document wastes valuable time. In fact, many office documents are best delegated to an assistant or secretary.

Example 4: If you think that an official and binding agreement is "just a piece of paper," try explaining your view to anyone who's been involved in a contract dispute (or is married).

Example 5: Sometimes, written communication (writing, photocopying, collating, sending, and reading) takes much longer than expected. Ask yourself if writing the message is the most effective means of communicating it. Perhaps the company grapevine or a face-to-face meeting or a departmental meeting can do a more adequate job.

Chapter 22

Presenting Yourself and Your Ideas: Mastering the Skills of a Presentation

According to Gerard Blair, author of *Starting to Manage: The Essentials Skills,* presenting information is one of the most important skills in management. Whenever conveying plans, thoughts, or ideas to the boss, the board, or to customers, in effect a presentation is being made. Seen in this way, presentations can be formal or informal, yet in either case the basic objective remains the same: to communicate effectively.

First, the bad news. **Presentations,** by their very nature, put a person on display. Much rides on them. They convey a speaker's ability to be decisive, creative, and inspirational. In doing so they reflect leadership and managerial skills. When giving a presentation a speaker must convince others of the merits of his or her proposal as well as project enough confidence (and evidence) to motivate these people into giving their support.

Now the good news. Presentations provide a chance to speak freely and show your stuff. When someone holds the stage an audience is bound by good manners to sit and listen, so, at least at the beginning, the speaker should have everyone's attention. Most audiences respond to speakers who radiate a relaxed, informal manner, so it isn't necessary to approach a presentation as though life hangs in the balance. Put another way, a presentation provides an ideal format to *be yourself.* Since presentations are also mediums that foment discussion, using them as such establishes a connection with the people a speaker will be working with or against. Although it may not be suitable to hold a conversation with an audience during a presentation, providing a question-and-answer session at the end allows others to get involved by raising issues, presenting alternative views, and generating valuable input.

THE ALL-IMPORTANT GOAL: COMMUNICATION

The two most important factors in any presentation are (1) effective communication and (2) connecting with the audience. The entire preparation and content of a presentation should therefore be molded around its audience. Everything from words to charts and graphs should convey thoughts and ideas *in a way that is understandable to the people who are going to hear and see them.* Don't be fooled into thinking that a new suit or haircut will win the day—the presentation's message *and having it remembered* are the most important selling points. As one colleague of mine put it, "The six Ps of a presentation are: Proper Planning Prevents Piss-Poor Performance." The following steps, however, do a more specific job of conveying the planning process. Keep in mind the adage that for every five minutes planned in front of an audience, approximately one hour of preparation time is needed.

Step 1: Formulate Objectives

The first order of business when giving presentations is to write down the precise objectives you hope to achieve. This can take the form of a simple statement of intent. For example, the purpose of a presentation may be to gain permission, obtain funds, get approval of an idea, sell a product, or motivate employees. Whatever the objective, it's best to stick to one per presentation. If you remain unfocused on what it is you hope to achieve, you probably won't achieve it.

Step 2: Identify the Audience

Consider the audience and determine how the objective can best be achieved through them. If the presentation takes into account *their* fears, concerns, wants, or needs, then you're well on the way to achieving your objective. Understanding an audience shows that you've prepared and that you're on their side. For example, if motivation is the objective and employees are uneasy about the new technology your company is investing in, focus your presentation on the training that will be provided, explaining that job losses are not part of the business's plan. In the same vein, if you want to sell your company's senior management on a new idea and they're worried about cost overruns, focus on the amount of money your idea will create or save.

Step 3: Format the Presentation

All presentations must be structured. If they're not, the audience will not be able to follow them. When addressing others it's wise to choose a format that best displays an objective without being too dull, obvious, or complicated. Here are some examples:

- *The sandwich board* contains a simple, beginning-middle-end format. An introduction leads to a basic summary of the objective, which is then followed by a conclusion. This type of format is best used for short presentations.
- *Subheadings (hierarchical)* break down the main topic into subtopics and those subtopics are broken down further. This technique is very effective when using written presentations or visual aids. In a verbal context, the objective of the presentation should be kept simple so as to avoid reducing the objective down to too many pieces.
- *The journalistic approach* introduces the topic in an opening paragraph, then hammers the point home in subsequent paragraphs that further elaborate on the basic presentation objective. This approach relies heavily on repetition and is enhanced by anecdotes, facts, and other relevant bits of information. When done well, this can really keep an audience entertained and online.
- *The question-answer method* explains a topic by introducing it and providing any relevant background information, then showing the topic's various advantages and disadvantages. During the summary, everything is listed as to its pros and cons and a discussion follows. The trick is for the presenter to provide the criteria on which all options are judged beforehand, thereby allowing the desired outcome to be achieved.

MAKING OR BREAKING A PRESENTATION

The Introduction

Most audiences are won or lost in the first few minutes of a presentation. To ensure starting off on the right foot, begin with these five elements in mind:

1. *Ensure that you're the center of attention.* Wait until everyone is seated and has made themselves comfortable. Be patient while they finish acknowledging the person seated next to them. An effective way to do this (if circumstances allow) is to stand at the front of the audience and politely smile until they have silenced (disciplined) themselves. This avoids having to ask that everyone be quiet, which can start a speaker off on the wrong foot.

2. *State your theme.* Get the audience thinking about the presentation's objective by opening with an anecdote, question, or simple statement that illustrates the subject matter.

3. *Outline how you wish to proceed.* Let the audience know what to expect. Not only does this allow them to follow the structure of the presentation, it also promises an end to it.

4. *Make the connection.* If the audience is won over in the first minute or two of the presentation, it should be possible to hold them much longer. This can be accomplished by presenting yourself as an expert, a concerned colleague, or even a friend. Many people think that starting with a joke is essential, but this can lead to disaster if the audience isn't known well. Use jokes only if doing so comes naturally and if the subject demands it.

5. *End with a bang.* The final impression you make (apart from your opening gambit) is probably what an audience will remember most vividly. Keep this in mind when preparing your introduction. As with your opening statement, it's always necessary to gather the audience's attention at the presentation's end. Try not to close with a summary. This switches people off very quickly. Instead, focus on the main objective and introduce one final culminating thought or idea that brings the message home.

Making the Pitch

Of all elements discussed or shown in a presentation, the person doing the speaking is usually what's remembered most. Every presenter has the power to either kill the message or enhance it. The following tools will help to facilitate success:

1. *Appearance:* The motto "dress for success" is key. A good rule of thumb is to be yourself and not dress over or under what your audience will be wearing. Doing so will only distance you from your listeners, and if you look out of place, you've lost the game before it begins.

2. *Stance:* Use your body as a tool. Don't appear too casual (bored) or overpowering (threatening). Keep your movements smooth and natural and keep them in unison with your speech. If you mention "togetherness," then bring your hands slowly together. If you want to emphasize a point or two, don't thrust an index finger at the audience but instead raise it toward the sky or *gently* bring your hand to the lectern. Waving your hands in the air and pacing rapidly back and forth are disruptive, and usually have no place in a presentation. Last, *always* stand erect, but don't remain as stiff as a statue.

3. *Eyes and expression:* Throughout any presentation, most audience members will be watching the presenter's face, or more specifically, his or her eyes. If the speaker is enthusiastic, knowledgeable, and generally happy, then the audience will feel this and respond appropriately. The same applies if the speaker is bored, listless, speaks in a monotone, or makes some other negative impact. The point is for the presenter to establish eye contact with as many people as possible. This contact should last for two or three seconds (long enough to acknowledge the recipient). If contact is too short, the speaker will appear flippant. If the contact is too long, aggressiveness enters the picture. When addressing a large group, attention should be paid equally to every section of the audience—few things are as maddening to an assembly as a speaker who only appears to care about one or two listeners. Finally (and perhaps most important), *smile*—not like the Cheshire cat, but in a relaxed and casual way.

4. *Visual aids:* Most people expect a formal presentation to be re-inforced with **visual aids** or slides. Since every presentation should be geared to what its audience wants, visual aids proba-bly need to be incorporated. The essential factor to remember is that pictures really do say a thousand words. Few things bring a point home more effectively than an appropriate illustration or stage prop. Bear in mind that a simple statement projected onto a screen can also be used in this context. For example, if your talk is about safety, projecting that word onto a screen should keep everyone focused on that issue. If your talk is about gener-ating profits, a picture of a pile of money may be effective (or it could be inappropriate—keep your audience's expectations in mind). Stage props such as models, examples of publications, or similar items can also highlight a topic. Just be sure they add to rather than distract from your message. Don't overburden your audience with too many words or pictures and don't think that visual aids will save a bad presentation. Ensure that every visual aid has a distinct purpose. If it doesn't, get rid of it.

5. *Common sense:* Most audiences are comprised of people who have a lot on their minds. Children, spouses, job responsibili-ties, doctor's appointments, debts—all these concerns and more present a potential distraction to your presentation. In order to prevent the audience's mind from wandering, keep your presen-tation short and to the point. This may sound like common sense, but common sense is often commonly ignored. Learn to crystallize your presentation in thirty seconds and you'll have the perfect ending or introduction from which to start. Equally as important, try not to use too many big words. Your audience will not be impressed.

6. *Repetition:* Make certain you present your point again and again without sounding like a parrot. To do this, repeat a point or reemphasize an issue utilizing different variations of what you've said. This allows people to better hear and understand your message. As author Gerard Blair says, the classic advice given by drill sergeants when addressing recruits is, "First tell 'em what you're going to tell 'em. Then tell 'em. Then tell 'em what you just told 'em!"

7. *Rehearsal:* Practice, practice, practice what you are going to say beforehand. If possible, give a trial run in front of others. If this

is not possible, practice in front of a mirror. Remember, practice *does* make perfect—but only when you make a positive effort to improve.

8. *Getting rid of the jitters:* It's normal and natural to feel nervous before giving a presentation. In fact, not being nervous is often a bad sign (overconfidence is a killer). The best ways to get a grip on too much nervousness are to
   - prepare well in advance—the more prepared you are the less chance there is of failure;
   - establish a genuine interest in what you're talking about—being enthusiastic about the subject of your presentation helps you focus on that rather than what you're doing; and
   - practice talking with and listening to people—the more time spent with people, the more accustomed you'll become in speaking to them collectively.

FINAL THOUGHTS

After the presentation is over and the audience has left, stop to think about what happened. Make a mental note of the high and low points. Ask others to provide feedback. Unless you make an effort to improve upon your weaknesses, you cannot realistically expect to make any future improvements.

Chapter 23

Making Meetings Matter

Although repetition is a necessary part of the learning process, the following information is not designed as a repeat of the previous three chapters. Instead, the objectives of this chapter are to (1) help determine if a **meeting** is necessary, (2) help with the meeting planning process, and (3) ensure meetings don't waste time.

More often than not, with the advent of easy-to-use color printers, eye-catching graphics, spreadsheet programs, and slide presentations, it's easy to lose sight of that fact that meetings are not supposed to merely convey information. That in itself can be accomplished by holding a conversation, using the phone, or writing a memo or e-mail. Instead, the purpose of business meetings is to be *task-oriented*. The idea is to achieve an objective that can be better obtained through group participation. The aim is to address an issue or set of issues and have everyone walk away with a viable solution (or at least be closer to one). Because this takes time and planning, too many routine meetings (those held at a specific time each week) are often cobbled together without much forethought, thereby becoming dreaded, ineffective, demoralizing, and time wasting. In fact, most meetings that don't have a preplanned, results-oriented objective often have the same effect.

TEN STEPS FOR PLANNING
A SUCCESSFUL MEETING

Before calling a meeting, focus on the following points:

1. *Necessity.* Think about your meeting's justification. Is it really necessary? Will anyone's time be wasted? What could better be done in place of a meeting?

2. *Purpose.* What is the meeting's purpose? What are its goals? What is the desired outcome? Keep in mind that all business meetings must be customer oriented. If you can't figure out how your meeting relates to customers, you're wasting valuable time.

3. *People.* Who is best suited to lead the meeting? Who needs to be in attendance? Who doesn't need to be there? How will the meeting's planners avoid offending people who aren't invited? How will they encourage those who are needed, but don't want to attend?

4. *Planning.* Has the appropriate research been conducted to call a meeting? (Meetings should rarely involve the input of only one person.) Is there enough material for a complete agenda?

5. *Preparation.* Will any premeeting information be properly distributed (a short description of the topic, an outline of what is expected to happen, references to any pertinent information, etc.) at least three days before the scheduled date of the meeting? *All participants* should know *exactly* what is expected of them.

6. *Tools.* Are all the items necessary to conduct a meeting available (projectors, computers, software, paper, pens, white boards, etc.)? Is all the needed equipment in good working order?

7. *Practice.* Are the people involved with conducting the meeting practicing their presentation(s)?

8. *Introduction.* Will the meeting start on time? Will it end on time? When it begins, is the chair prepared to restate its purpose as well as the rules or procedures everyone is expected to follow? Will a rundown be provided on who will have the floor?

9. *Brainstorming.* After the initial presentations have ended, will the chair move quickly toward the brainstorming part of the meeting? (This is usually the reason why most meetings are called.) Is the chair (or someone else) prepared to write down conclusions, assign responsibilities, and determine time limitations? Will an appropriate amount of time be made available for a question-and-answer segment? Will the meeting conclude with a summarizing of the discussion, a restating of the conclusions, and a going over of the agreed-upon next step(s)?

10. *Follow-up*. Will everyone receive a copy of the meeting's minutes? Who will ensure that whatever has been agreed upon will be completed? Who will monitor or measure the meeting's results? How will this be done?

When it comes to meetings, the moral of the story, as with so much in management, is that adequate planning, examination, and follow-through are the essential elements behind success. If the previous ten steps are used and a positive answer can be found for most of the questions raised, you should be well on the way toward making your meetings productive, enlightening, and—miracle of miracles—perhaps even anticipated.

Chapter 24

An Outline for Project or Program Planning

In every field, the progress of today is nothing more than the absurdity of yesterday.

Luigi Barzini,
Corriere della Sera (1910)

Imagine being handed a choice assignment at work that requires you to journey into uncharted territory. What will you do?

By its very nature, management constantly asks that people learn to do new things as well as familiar things in different ways. This can be frightening because planning, developing, and implementing new ideas and methods (venturing into the unknown) is usually a daunting process. But cheer up. It can be tackled. People do it every day. As with any large task, breaking down what needs to be done into manageable units is a good way to get started. Before beginning any new **project,** though, it's mandatory to do one thing first: the planning. The following outline should prove helpful.

I. Why? Before starting, clearly understand *why* you're doing whatever it is you're doing. This helps to define your task by explaining both the problem and, to some degree, the proposed solution. The result should be a *written* guideline describing what's needed as well as why and when. Bear in mind that everyone involved must be in agreement. If the crucial first step of writing everything down and agreeing with it isn't done, you'll pay dearly for it later. There are several reasons why this is so:

A. Agreeing in advance helps eliminate contradictory assumptions. In business you should never assume a common understanding because you'll probably be wrong. All it takes for a project to hit the skids is one new member (or manager) who is uninformed or not in agreement and the process may have to start all over again.

B. An agreement forces all concerned to read and think about what's being proposed. This includes setting reasonable time scales, deliveries, and so forth.

C. Written agreements help clarify issues and/or reveal misunderstandings, particularly with other departments or people.

D. A solid agreement helps expose practical and technical details as well as identify resources that will be needed (and perhaps the authority to use them).

E. Agreements help prevent people from changing their minds or coming up with new ideas halfway through the project (which almost always results in increases in cost and time).

F. Written specifications reveal the big picture by showing how everything fits together, thereby helping illuminate incompatibilities, inconsistencies, and duplications.

II. What? The *what* stage brings a project into focus by beginning the process at the point at which needs and ideas are joined together. The key word here is *structure*. Without structure, any project will become a tangled mess of seemingly unrelated tasks. By using your experience (and the experience of others) you should, at the very least, be able to make an educated guess for each of the following questions. *Don't attempt the planning process on your own.* A manager's duty is not to single-handedly come up with all the answers but to use everyone at his or her disposal to come up with the best possible solutions.

A. Objectives
    1. What exactly do our customers want or need?
    2. How do we wish to serve them?
    3. What exactly do we (and our business) hope to accomplish?
    4. What are our financial capabilities? Our estimated labor needs? Equipment requirements?
    5. What will be the long-term effects of the project or program?

B. What Methods Will Be Used to Gain Our Objectives?
 1. What types of communication (or controls) will be used? How often will they be used?
 2. What type of management/organizational structures are most appropriate?
C. What Realistic Time Frames Will Be Set (or Have Been Set for Us)?
 1. What is the best time to start and finish each of the project's segments?
 2. Can clear, unambiguous, "milestone" targets be set?
 3. Are there any conflicts with other projects/dates/schedules?
 4. Are we being too optimistic or restrictive with our time estimations?
 5. Can certain segments be lumped together for maximum effect?
 6. Should segments be broken down further to facilitate successful completion?
D. Who Should Lead the Different Segments of the Project?
 1. Who is the best person for each job?
 2. How will people develop in their assignments?
 3. Should tasks be handled individually, in pairs, or in teams?
 4. Will we have to hire additional staff?
 5. Should tasks be handled in-house or will they be better accomplished through outside contractors?
III. How? The *how* phase constitutes the real-time planning of the project. This is the stage at which the manager sits down with his or her team and starts the process of actually managing. Continuing to obtain the feedback of others helps ensure that fewer mistakes will be made and allows for group ownership in the final plan. Again, remember that nothing can be assumed here (you will probably be wrong) and *everything must be put into writing and agreed upon*. The object at this stage is to establish the monitoring of the project and provide for a system that allows for the receiving of any early danger warnings. In doing so, the foundation for cooperation, as well as motivation, is fortified. Throughout, you must instill the notion that your team(s) is

responsible for monitoring and controlling its own progress via tangible forms of measurement.

A. Financing the Project
   1. Have full costs been determined and necessary revenues been developed?
   2. Have financial resources been properly allocated?
B. Accumulation of Resources
   1. What type of people, equipment, facilities, schedules, and materials are needed?
   2. What type of training do the project's people and/or team(s) need?
   3. What are the project's insurance requirements?
   4. Have legalities, liabilities, and legal waivers been determined?
C. Distribution of Assignments
   1. Have we selected, consulted, and appointed the best person(s) for each job?
   2. Have the best outside contractors, suppliers, etc. been selected?
   3. Do we know when to make compromises?
   4. Have the standards of what constitutes quality been agreed upon?
   5. Have safety and ethical concerns been addressed?
   6. Have alternatives been penciled in or discussed?
D. Establishment of Communication Pathways
   1. When and how should problems and updates be reported?
   2. Who is responsible to whom?
E. Final Agreements
   1. Does everyone know about his or her duties, responsibilities, and contingency plans?
   2. Are current or foreseen problems being fixed or adjusted?
   3. Has reasonable time been scheduled for errors? (Don't fall into the trap of assuming that nothing will go wrong.)
IV. When? At last, you've started the ball rolling. The project is underway. Be attentive to what is going on and expect the unexpected. Keep in mind that when something does go wrong (which it inevitably will), the best way to approach the problem

is to not immediately ask *why* it happened, but rather *how it can be corrected.*

A. Moving Forward
1. A point has been set on the horizon; now move toward it (keep in mind the old joggers' adage that the hardest step to take is always the first one out the door).
2. Stay informed as to what is going on without satisfying the desire to look over everyone's shoulder.
3. Provide and receive adequate feedback (including lots of praise and/or professional criticism and correction when needed).
4. Allow for flexibility.
5. Be patient and reasonable, and remember that any form of progress, no matter how small, is progress.
6. Self-doubt and momentary lapses of confidence are normal—just don't let them consume you or your team.

B. Quality Control
1. Are the project's people meeting the agreed-upon quality standards?
2. Should any changes be made?
3. Are any of the suggested changes really necessary? (Too many changes will slow your project down and add to its costs.)

C. Fighting for Time
1. If you find yourself falling behind schedule, *find out why* and *correct the problem immediately.*
2. If senior managers move a deadline forward and it can't be met, remind them of the original schedule and try for a compromise solution rather than flat-out saying no.

V. How did it go? After the project or program has been completed a review of what happened and the lessons learned should be made. This is best done in an open meeting through candid discussion and should include as many internal and external customers as possible. Summing up *always* proves invaluable and will help keep you on track in the pursuit of what should be the reason behind every project or program: increased customer satisfaction.

PART IV:
THE BASICS OF BUSINESS

Chapter 25

Know Your Product

A timid man fears being bullied. As a result, he signs up for karate lessons at a local martial arts school. For three years he steadfastly sticks to the program, never missing a lesson. Day by day his confidence grows until, shortly after he graduates, a mugger demanding his wallet confronts him. The man strikes the classic kung fu pose, overjoyed at finally gaining control over his life. But his display is in vain. The mugger shrugs, pulls out a gun, and shoots him.

The message? Information, skills, and training are wonderful acquirements, but they aren't applicable to every situation. Equally as important, some situations aren't always as straightforward as they seem. **Products** are one example.

PRODUCT LEVELS

Every manager should be aware that every product (or service) has three distinct levels (see also Figure 25.1):

1. The *core product:* the actual benefit that consumers receive when they purchase a product.
2. The *actual product:* the attributes that separate one product from another in terms of quality, features, design, packaging, and so on.
3. The *augmented product:* additional services and benefits incorporated with the core product, such as installation, warranty, delivery, credit, or after-sales service.

Success in business greatly relies on finding out which level of a product is the most appealing to customers and then adjusting all pol-

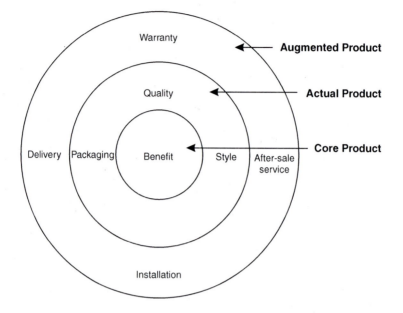

FIGURE 25.1. Product (or Service) Levels

icies and procedures accordingly in order to target specific customer groups and maximize sales.

The **core product** of McDonald's, for example, might be convenience (which is why so many McDonald's restaurants have great locations). Or it could be uniformity, hygiene, fast service, price, or some other *benefit* a patron *seeks* when choosing to eat there. The **actual product** is the burgers, fries, and foodstuffs. However, the next time you see a McDonald's advertisement, notice how little is said about the taste of the food. Instead, the **augmented product** is often used to make a sale, usually a coupon or movie tie-in taking the form of a toy that entices customers (or their children) into the restaurant.

Alternatively, the core product of a cosmetics company might be hope, sex appeal, sophistication, beauty, image, or whatever else it is that customers think cosmetics provide. This is then emphasized in a marketing campaign that focuses on youth, fighting age, career success, sassiness, sex appeal, trendiness, etc. The actual product, which is wrapped around the core product, is the brand name and physical product (lipstick, blush, mascara, etc.). The augmented product could be a money-back guarantee, a free sample, or something along similar lines that creates perceived extra value.

Which Product Level Results in the Most Sales?

Many experts concede that most business competition takes place at the augmented benefit level. The problem for managers is that augmented products (i.e., the added value in the form of freebies) have a tendency to become expected over time—and that costs money. A good example of this is British Airways wanting to place a small chocolate on the trays of its passenger meals to provide something a bit more special, but when a cost analysis was done, it was determined that this simple gesture would cost more than 1.5 million dollars a year!

UNDERSTANDING WHAT YOUR CUSTOMERS WANT

Years ago, while living in Nottingham, England, I watched a friend, a city center gym owner, as he struggled through a minor dilemma. As a small business manager with limited funds, he wanted to make certain that the $3,000 ad he was placing in the local yellow pages directory would attract customers. He had narrowed his decision to four different styles when he asked for my input. "Which one do you think is best?" he asked.

"It doesn't matter what I think," I replied. "What your customers think is more important. Do you know the reason why they chose this gym over the other ones in town?"

He shook his head and shrugged. "Convenience?" he suggested.

"Why don't you ask them?" I said. Before he could reply, I spread the four ads on the top of the reception desk and asked a woman signing in to select the one she thought was best. I then asked what had attracted her to the gym in the first place. During the following thirty minutes I did the same with each person that either entered or left. Far from being taken aback, everyone absolutely relished being asked for their opinion. Soon a line of persons had formed, each eager to give his or her input. In the end, more than 90 percent of them chose one ad as the most eye-catching, but more important, all of them mentioned price as the number one reason for joining. Incredibly, my friend hadn't mentioned price or value in any of his ads, so he took the selected advertisement back to the yellow pages and had BEST PRICES IN TOWN placed at the top in bold print. Since he now knows his core product is price and value, that's what he has to keep providing. Eventually this may change (customer wants usually do), but for now he knows what to focus on.

Sometimes It's Just So Simple

In 1997, I journeyed to Glasgow, Scotland, to investigate a PhD program into which I'd been accepted (I decided to write a novel instead). While there I spent a delightful afternoon listening to a man whose work provided most of the funding for one of the university's graduate schools. His office, literally piled to the ceiling with stacks of papers, was located in an ancient building's attic on the university campus. I immediately fell in love with the place. It was the office of a true business practitioner. "Why on earth do you want a PhD?" he asked in his thick Scottish accent. "Come work here with me instead."

For an hour or so we swapped stories about our work experiences. One of his better tales concerned a local museum that regularly lost money at its food service operation. For a time, the university sent dozens of graduate students and professors to research the problem, but despite their lengthy questionnaires and complicated data collections no firm conclusions were reached. That's when he decided to pay a visit. "Within a few minutes of arriving I knew exactly what the problem was," he explained, "it was the tables. The only option available to customers were long tables that everyone had to use together. Needless to say, most people don't want to sit among groups of complete strangers, so they ended up bypassing this area and going somewhere else to get a cup of tea."

He then suggested to the museum's management that they get rid of the long tables and buy smaller, more intimate ones. Soon after, the area filled up and began making money. "It all came down to providing what most people want after walking around all day looking at exhibits," he said, "and that is a few minutes of rest and calm. Tea and cake is an afterthought—it's the relaxation people want. Yet how can they do that if they're forced to share a table with a group of screaming schoolchildren?"

CONFRONTING COMPETITION

Being aware of your business's core product, actual product, and augmented product can help provide formidable ammunition against major competitors. But what can a local mom-and-pop grocery do to beat a Wal-Mart superstore opening just down the road? How can a hamburger stand take on a giant such as McDonald's? What can a local photocopying center do when a new Office Depot opens across the street? For the most part, you must know exactly what *benefits* customers need or want. More often than not, the way to successfully compete against a major rival, regardless of its size, is to offer what it can't—and that usually translates into individualized customer service. For example, my friend in the Nottingham gym story discussed earlier has been in business for seventeen years. During that time, six other fitness facilities have come and gone, yet his business keeps chugging along. The reason it does so becomes clear the moment you walk in the door and either he, or someone else on his staff, greets you as if you were a long lost friend. Simply put, customers are made to feel as if they belong, which plays a major role in customer retention. What's more, this type of focused, personalized service doesn't cost anything. His core product, as we saw, is price and value. His actual product though, apart from the gym itself, is service. From time to time he also runs sales and specials (particularly to students and groups) that many would classify as an augmented product.

In another example, a colleague of mine once relayed how a local photocopying center in his town was able to stay in business despite the existence of an Office Depot that opened across the street. Desperate to stay in the game, the small business owner decided to provide as many new services as possible that his rival couldn't, such as free pick up and delivery, while eliminating the retail side of his business with which he couldn't hope to compete.

Yet another tale is told about a small retail shop that found itself going head to head against a new Wal-Mart superstore. Rather than admit defeat, the small business owner cased his bigger rival and found out (1) specific products it didn't sell and (2) products it didn't sell well. After studying the buying habits of his customers, he then transformed his business to provide what Wal-Mart didn't. The result was that he became a local specialist in hardware and cleaning supplies—something Wal-Mart simply did not want to do.

Last, a host of small-time food stands competes against McDonald's and every other world-class fast-food restaurant in Warsaw, Poland, by providing what the big guns can't—*very* low prices. With hardly any overheads, these small businesses attract enough customers to pull a tidy profit, and none of the bigger chains can touch them.

KNOW YOUR MARKET

Ultimately, it's up to each business to find out exactly what its customers want and then decide the best means to deliver those needs (see Chapter 28, "Tools for Developing External and Internal Customers"). Knowing that every product has three distinct levels can provide a new perspective on what is being sought and what is being sold. Just as important, providing these benefits doesn't have to add substantially to a business's overheads. All it takes is a sincere desire to improve, a little common sense, the ability to listen (an open mind), and plenty of creativity. But be warned, because just like the man who thought many of his troubles would evaporate if he learned karate, if you don't know your customer's exact wants and needs you may end up doing your business more harm than good.

Chapter 26

Competitive Advantage Strategy

Strategy is not about predicting the future; it's about using the here and now to *prepare* for the future. In a business sense, this means developing an edge over rivals in order to secure customers and defend against competitors. In other words, strategy means creating a competitive advantage.

TYPES OF STRATEGIES

Generally speaking, there are three types of **competitive advantage** strategy:

1. A *low-cost strategy* strives to offer the lowest prices in town. The intent is to attract a broad cross section of the market. Low-cost strategies usually depend on offering few frills, having a limited selection, and extolling a somewhat acceptable quality. In a company that opts for a low-cost strategy, the emphasis is on continually seeking to keep costs down, year after year, in every aspect of the business, without sacrificing quality altogether. In the marketplace a focus is made on trying to make a virtue out of the product's features that lead to low prices. Of course, low prices are an extremely valuable asset when attracting consumers because, in part, it costs little for consumers to switch to a low-cost product line. In addition, standardized products can and do satisfy the needs of many customers, but these advantages can be neutralized if a competitor adopts similar low-cost methods. Similarly, concentrating on low costs can divert attention from other important aspects of a product that are dependant on the changing tastes of customers.

2. A *differentiation strategy* seeks to broaden customer choice by selling different variations of the same product. The *aim* is to attract a broad cross section of the market via the ability to offer variety (for

example, Procter & Gamble makes at least nine types of laundry detergents to satisfy its customers' different needs). The idea is to provide value for buyers by building in whatever differences customers want (such as quality). The company's goal therefore, is to communicate these differences in credible ways while charging a premium price since creating a line of different products usually results in higher costs. The manager's job is to stress constant improvement, invest in innovation, and concentrate on each product's distinct features. Doing so helps create buyer loyalty, but only if the company fully understands what customers consider as valuable. In other words, customers must see a distinct advantage with differentiated products or they'll go for lower priced alternatives.

3. A *focus* or *"niche" strategy* concentrates on a narrow part of a market rather than the whole market. The idea is to sell to a specific clientele whose preferences are known to be distinctly different from the rest of the market. The advantage of this is that lower costs are usually associated with serving a niche. The company's goal is to communicate the product's unique ability to its targeted buyers. A manager's job when using this strategy is to remain totally dedicated to serving the niche better than competitors while not damaging the company's image by selling out to other markets. The main reason for adopting a niche strategy is because big competitors don't usually like to cater to small markets. But make no mistake, if a niche market proves profitable, the big companies *will* move in. Examples of businesses using niche strategies include: easyJet airline company and Charles Schwab investment services.

Which Strategy Is Best?

Whenever I lecture about competitive strategy students inevitably ask why a company can't choose all three options. The answer is because it's *very* difficult for an organization to be all things to all people. For example, imagine three different career options: writer, athlete, and lawyer. As with any career choice, the literary world is full of competition. In fact, the odds of making a living as a writer are actually worse than winning the lottery. To put it mildly, it takes years of focused dedication, talent (or luck), and some form of interim financial backing to succeed as a writer. Now imagine a person who not only wants to become a writer, but also a professional athlete. If that isn't enough, try to visualize this same person wanting to become a lawyer too. Absurd? Absolutely. Each career option simply takes too much time, money, focus, and effort on its own. The same holds true for businesses when formulating a competitive strategy. Yes, some companies do succeed using two or three strategies, but they're the exception rather than the rule. The rest of us have enough on our hands just focusing on one.

Sometimes a Good Strategy Is So Obvious You Can't See It

Two hikers are walking through the woods. The first hears a noise, looks up, and sees a large, angry bear charging toward him. He turns to warn his colleague, only to find him sitting on a rock and putting on a pair of running shoes. "Are you crazy?" shouts the first hiker. "You can't outrun a bear!"

"I don't have to outrun the bear," the second hiker calmly replies. "I just have to outrun you."

As this joke suggests, good strategy can be both obvious and simple. For example, Canon's photocopying division used the phrase "beat Xerox" to describe its product differentiation strategy, and Wal-Mart, in its early days, stated that it simply wanted to "overtake Sears" via a low-cost competitive advantage. In Japan, a large construction-vehicle manufacturer named Komatsu made clear its strategic intent when it announced that it wanted to "encircle Caterpillar" with a broader product line.

The Ten Commandments of Business Strategy

1. Always think in the long term.
2. Never get stuck in the pack with no distinctive competitive position.
3. Always invest in a clear, proper, sustainable competitive advantage.
4. Avoid strategies that will succeed only in the best of circumstances.
5. Show caution when pursuing a rigidly prescribed or inflexible strategy—changing conditions may render it obsolete.
6. Never underestimate the reaction and commitment of rivals.

7. Remember that attacking a competitor's weakness is usually more profitable than attacking its strengths.
8. Don't cut prices without establishing a firm cost advantage over rivals.
9. Don't start something (a price war, a marketing offer, a new service, etc.) that you can't afford or stop.
10. Beware of attacking larger, stronger rivals without adequate resources. (Thompson and Strickland, 1993)

MATCHING STRATEGY TO THE BUSINESS

For any business, a winning strategy is the one that best matches the style and capabilities of the company with the wants and needs of its customers. Although that may sound patently obvious, it's based on the concept that a business must sell what customers want—not what the business wants to sell. How is this best done? Through the topics presented in Chapters 1 through 32 of this book. All of the principles and techniques mentioned in these chapters help lay the groundwork for business success. Again, strategy is about *preparing* for the future, not trying to predict it. The only way to prepare for the future is to strengthen your weaknesses (and those of your business), hone up on as many skills as possible, and remain adaptive and responsive to whatever is thrown your way.

Chapter 27

The Importance of Marketing

In 1991, only two companies in the world manufactured a special type of industrial flexible pipe. One was located in the United States, the other in France. Competition between the two companies was fierce. Then the Gulf War broke out, and it was quickly discovered that the products these companies made were perfect for helping to put out the oil-rig fires ignited by Saddam Hussein's fleeing forces. Soon both companies could barely keep up with demand.

Around this time one of the American company's young administrators, freshly armed with an MBA in finance (from Harvard), convinced his grandfather (who sat on the board of directors) that he could do a better job managing the company than the current team. In due course the old man persuaded the other board members that his grandson would take the company to a whole new level. That he did. Shortly after being named as the new president, the grandson decided to cut costs by eliminating a third of the workforce—including the *entire* sales and marketing department. To add insult to injury, guards with 9mm pistols were brought in on the day the pink slips were handed out to ensure any resultant anger didn't get out of hand. A year later he sat back scratching his head wondering why the company hadn't sold anything. How on earth could someone entrusted with running a company (and with a Harvard MBA to boot) be so stupid?

THE BASICS OF MARKETING

Hopefully by this point in the book you have arrived at the conclusion that few elements are more important to a business than marketing and sales. Contrary to popular belief, if you build a better mousetrap the world will not beat a path to your door. Just as important, good products do not sell themselves. One heart-wrenching situation I clearly remember involved watching a man (the first person to take a chance and hire me in my then chosen profession) lament the fact that he couldn't make a success of his enterprise despite it being a top-of-the-line establishment that stood head and shoulders above its competitors. "When I built this place," he told me, "I thought people would be lining up outside the door." His words, and the mournful way he stated them, still send a shiver down my spine to this day.

Marketing is a complex subject whose breadth makes it difficult to define. In essence, it involves *everything* an organization does. It's purpose however, is to bring a buyer and a seller together. Everything within a business plays its part in either encouraging or preventing marketing from happening. The product itself, its advertising, the way phones are answered, the cleanliness of an establishment, the training of employees, the sale, and everything afterward and in between, all comprise the basis of marketing.

THE MARKETING MIX

The most popular way to explain the multiple facets of marketing is to break the subject up into sections through an alliteration called the marketing mix, which includes the following:

- *Product:* the benefit of what is being sold or produced
- *Place:* the location (or time) where the product is sold or distributed
- *Price:* the perceived value of the product
- *Promotion:* communicating the product to potential customers
- *People:* the employees (and their knowledge or training) who make and/or sell the product
- *Physical environment:* the ambience or physical interior in which the product is sold
- *Processes:* the operational services that keep an organization running smoothly

The purpose of the marketing mix is to section the business into workable pieces that can be milled and sharpened in order to satisfy customers. Knowing what customers want beforehand helps identify opportunities. These opportunities are then researched to uncover any strengths or weaknesses and the results are matched with the business's abilities. The completed process is then targeted to a segment of the market in which success is envisioned because scattershot approaches are often highly ineffective. As seen in Chapter 25, "Know Your Product," marketers should focus on **benefit perception** (i.e., the benefits perceived by a potential customer), because all customers weigh in their minds the benefits they believe can be obtained by buying a product. They then act accordingly—if managers and employees are ready and able to finalize a sale.

THE PROMOTION MIX

Companies usually get their message to customers across via the promotion mix:

I. **Advertising** is any paid form of a nonpersonal presentation and promotion of a product.
   A. Pros
      1. It's a creative medium and its message can be repeated several times.
      2. It can be used diversely: from building up a long-term image to triggering quick sales.
      3. It can reach masses of people at a low cost per exposure.
      4. Consumers tend to view advertised products as legitimate.
      5. Large-scale advertising says something positive about a company's size and success.
   B. Cons
      1. It's impersonal and isn't necessarily persuasive.
      2. It carries only a one-way conversation with its audience.
      3. It can be very costly and ineffective if the wrong advertising medium is used. (One of the better lines from the world of marketing comes from a manager who stated, "I know half my budget is wasted on advertising; I just don't know which half!")
II. **Personal selling** is the use of oral presentation with one or more prospective customers for the purpose of making a sale and building a relationship.

    A. Pros
       1. It involves personal interaction between two or more people so the needs and characteristics of a buyer can be determined quickly.
       2. It can create a relationship that leads to further sales.
       3. A buyer usually feels a greater need to listen and respond to a real live person.
    B. Cons
       1. It can cost a lot to hire, train, and maintain a good sales force.
       2. It involves a long-term commitment (advertising can be turned on and off, but a sales force takes time to hire and train).

III. **Sales promotions** are short-term incentives designed to encourage the purchase of a product. Examples include coupons, contests, price reductions, offers, two-for-one-deals, and free samples.
    A. Pros
       1. They attract immediate customer attention.
       2. They offer incentives to purchase or try a product by adding value for customers.
       3. They invite and reward quick response.
    B. Cons
       1. They're short-lived and usually not effective in building long-run brand preference.

IV. **Public relations** (PR) is the building of good relations with the public by obtaining favorable publicity and creating a good image. This includes handling (or heading off) unfavorable rumors, stories, and events.
    A. Pros
       1. It's very believable—PR news stories, features, and events seem real and convincing.
       2. It can reach those who avoid salespeople since the message gets to its audience as "news" rather than a sales pitch.
    B. Cons
       1. PR can turn into a management nightmare if the company begins to believe its own PR, imagines that it's untouchable, and lowers its guard.

PRODUCT LIFE CYCLE

No matter how new or wonderful a product is, it will eventually go through phases akin to childhood, midlife, and old age. This is called **product life cycle.** Each phase requires a different marketing approach. Products can also "die" unless counteracted by an effective marketing campaign. In a product's introduction stage, advertising, promotion, and public relations are sometimes best for producing awareness. Personal selling, if used, might be geared toward convincing traders to carry the product or in attracting the interest of large centralized groups (such as clubs, professional organizations, companies, etc.). In the growth stage, advertising and promotion should probably dominate. In the mature stage, buyers are probably aware of the product and therefore may only need reminding, so advertising tends to cover the bill (although promotion can be used to boost interest and sales). In the decline stage, advertising is usually kept at a reminder level as promotions take over. However, since marketing should ultimately be customer led, any combination of the promotion mix may prove to be suitable at any time.

Increasing a Product's Marketing Life

One method of prolonging a product's life is to look at the product in different ways, based on the following viewpoints:

- *Uses:* This involves adapting (or promoting) different uses for a product. For example, a fitness center can use its aerobic studio for karate classes. Baking soda is marketed as being useful for cooking, cleaning, and refreshing refrigerator interiors (as well as teeth). But the classic case has to be the 1950s Colgate toothpaste advertising campaigns that stated that using Colgate freshens breath. Of course all toothpastes freshen breath, but no other company had ever said this before in their advertising. As a result of voicing this additional benefit Colgate's sales soared.
- *Users:* This involves increasing a product's appeal by targeting it to different groups. For example, I once worked at a resort that literally took the equipment from its outdoor children's camp activities and used them in corporate teamwork-promotion programs. In addition, variations of our exercise programs were

geared toward the fitness conscious (amateur athletes) and the health conscious (heart attack victims, the obese, and so on).

• *Usage:* This involves getting the customer to use a product more. The classic example is the instruction to "lather, rinse, repeat" on shampoo labels that supposedly resulted in double the product's usage overnight.

SOME MARKETING TIPS

Don't Go It Alone

There's no way around it: No business can succeed without selling something and sellers *must* search for buyers. In the process, the needs and wants of buyers must be determined and good products must be designed, promoted, delivered, stored, and their image constantly improved. It's an endless process, but there's no need to reinvent the wheel when marketing your business and selling your products. Information is widely available (much of it from the companies that make, sell, or distribute goods used in your business) as to how to attract buyer interest, display goods to maximum effect, and finalize a sale. Kraft, for example, sends representatives to show shop owners what products sell best according to local demographics as well as how to arrange cheeses and other products to maximize sales. The degree of accuracy regarding this type of information can be astonishing. In London, I once watched a news team challenge three marketers who claimed that they could determine a shopper's gender, age, profession, and first name (!) simply by looking at what the shopper had purchased. The marketers were then given three piles of goods and told to back up their claim. Forty minutes later, they correctly identified each shopper's sex, age, profession, and first name.

Marketing Doesn't Require Fancy Schemes or Costly Expenses

One of the best compliments I've ever been paid came from a friend who overheard a conversation in a shop. One of my competitors, a woman who'd been in business for twenty-five years, had earlier greeted my arrival in town with what can only be described via the words, "so what?" Six months later, I'd wrested most of her customers (and potential customers) away from her. "I've been here most of my life," she angrily told the shopkeeper, "yet now wherever I go I'm told that Jonathan Scott was here first."

Incredibly, I beat her in the marketplace with no advertising budget, no sales staff, no structured marketing campaigns, and—prepare yourself—no telephones (at the time we weren't accessible to a phone network). Realizing my limitations, I studied the programs we offered (an equestrian center, a sports club, a restaurant, and a golf course under construction) and did a great deal of research on potential customers. I then spent most of my free time visiting and introducing myself to consulates and embassies, local schools, apartment buildings, neighborhood community centers, and other places where people regularly gathered. You may find this hard to believe, but none of the other managers in the area, and there were quite a few, had ever done this before. Poster advertisements was about as far as they'd gone. Through repeated personal contact and the setting up of programs specifically designed for each targeted group *by* each targeted group, I established a client base that stuck with me through thick and thin as the business grew. Yes, we eventually got telephones, hired more staff, and printed fancy brochures, but our success was solidified through personal service and countless handshakes that cost no more than time, shoe leather, and elbow grease. The message couldn't be clearer. Today, marketing should be considered less of a broadcast medium and more of a customer-oriented dialogue.

Chapter 28

Tools for Developing External and Internal Customers

ESTABLISHING AN EXTERNAL CUSTOMER DATABASE

A good way to do more than pay lip service to servicing external customers is to establish a **customer database.** A database enables a business to study customer buying behavior and determine what may be needed in the future. Gathering this type of data is crucial, as is making it accessible. Working in their own departments, salespeople, accountants, and managers may not be aware of the whole customer picture, but working together they should be able to put one together. As always, if the answers to questions in the database are unknown— *ask the customer.* This is best accomplished through attentive contact that flatters customers by making them feel important. It needn't be (and shouldn't be) an interrogation. As with most good management practices, setting up a customer database isn't complicated (software programs are available). Most are quite simple and look similar to the following:

1. Customer specifics
   - Name, address, age, gender, profession, etc.
   - Geographic location and/or demographics of their business
   - Economic information (such as income level)
   - Basic needs and requirements
2. Purchasing history
   - Long term or short term
   - Amount purchased
   - Brand loyalty
   - Reason for buying (price, convenience, spur of the moment decision, etc.)

3. Future prospects
   - What are the customer's future plans?
   - What might he/she/they need in the future?
   - What type of future expenditures is the customer likely to make?
4. Other pertinent questions
   - How did the customer hear about us?
   - What does the customer need that we currently don't offer?
   - How can our service be improved?

MONITORING YOUR INTERNAL CUSTOMERS

Checking Progress: Evaluating Job Performance

Job evaluations are a valuable tool because they let employees know if they're going in the right direction and are doing what is expected of them. No evaluation style is superior; the varieties are endless and form should follow function. However, all evaluations should be written legibly to reflect seriousness on the part of the administrator as well as to have something substantial on file. Against this future progress can be measured. Also, don't look at evaluations as being negative. If they're done on a regular basis they're difficult to turn into reprimand sessions. When things are going well, they're also an excellent way to reward good performance. Just remember to keep them simple.

Work evaluations should take into consideration:

- Overall job performance
- Work output and quality
- Views from colleagues
- Social skills (including attitude toward work and co-workers)
- Punctuality and attendance
- Sometimes, the views or opinions of the person being evaluated

Work evaluations should avoid:

- Judgment on just one trait (good or bad)
- The ignoring of past performance by only judging recent work standards (this keeps the employee from "pouring on the goods" right before evaluation time)

- Personal bias
- Grading
- Marking everyone as average

Dealing with Consistently Poor Performance

When faced with an employee who shows consistently poor performance, find the answers to the following questions. All too often the blame for poor employee performance lays squarely on a manager's shoulders, and should therefore be rectifiable.

- Does the employee have a reason for his or her poor performance?
- Has proper training been provided?
- Is the employee being subjected to bullying by colleagues?
- Have proper motivational tactics and/or incentives been administered?
- Is the employee suffering from outside (personal) pressures?
- Is the employee working in a suitable department, field, or area?
- Is some form of punishment necessary? (*Note:* **Termination** is not a punishment. The process of firing an employee for poor performance is an act of finality that should be done only when all else has failed.)

A STITCH IN TIME SAVES NINE

Remember the old fable about the ant and the grasshopper? During the summer months the gadabout grasshopper sat back and laughed at the industrious ant. Then winter set in. Naturally, only the ant survived the cold because he had prepared for it. Likewise, whether your focus is on internal or external customers, forethought and effort will reap dividends. Proactivity is the key. With external customers, an updated customer database helps build a foundation from which further sales and contacts can be derived. With internal customers, keeping written records provides the measurement and information needed to develop your employees as well as possibly protect them (and you). The moral of the story couldn't be simpler: The work you do now may save your business in the future.

Chapter 29

Pricing

A dog walks into a bar and orders a beer. The bartender stares at the dog for a moment then gets him his order. "That'll be ten dollars," the bartender says. The dog produces the money from a pouch attached to his collar. "Sorry for staring," says the bartender, "but I have to admit that we don't get too many talking dogs in here."

"At these prices," says the dog, "I'm not surprised."

A *price* is the amount of money charged for a product or service, or the sum of values consumers exchange for the benefits of acquiring a product. Note the difference between price and value. *Price* is the monetary sum assigned to a product. *Value* is a customer's perception and may involve unseen costs such as the amount of money or time involved in switching over to your product.

Historically, prices for most goods were usually set through barter or negotiation. Prices therefore varied depending on a buyer's and seller's skills. However, in the early part of the twentieth century, F. W. Woolworth changed that by adopting a one-price policy in his stores. The practice soon spread.

FACTS ABOUT PRICING

- Price is the only component of the marketing mix that produces revenue. All others represent costs.
- Price is the most flexible element of the marketing mix. Unlike the other components, a price can be changed quickly.
- Pricing is often the most significant factor affecting buyer choice, but it's a double-edged sword. If a price is too high, buyers may turn away. If it's too low, they may sense something is wrong.

- Pricing often is not handled well (cut a price 10 percent and 50 percent of profits may be lost).

Common Mistakes in Pricing

- Setting prices that are too cost-oriented (i.e., customer value is not contemplated)
- Setting prices that do not reflect the current market (there could be high demand or a lack of demand)
- Not taking into account the other marketing mix components (again, the perception customers have of value may not be contemplated or may be misjudged)
- Not varying prices according to different products, different market segments, and/or promotions
- Slashing prices in the assumption that it will raise sales (the problem could be ineffective marketing, low perceived quality, or any number of other factors)
- Raising prices to increase revenues (again, the problem may lie somewhere else—and if it does, it won't be solved by upping prices and putting off customers)

THE PRICING PROCESS

Getting Started

Before the pricing process begins, it's necessary to consider what you want pricing to do for your business. The obvious answer is to generate revenue, but how will this be achieved? By being more competitive? By attracting a specific clientele? By getting more customers to try your products? A combination of one or more of these objectives? If you're serious enough about making the most of prices, then it's worth the time and effort to think about these questions, write them down, and discuss them with your colleagues.

Internal and External Factors Affecting Pricing

I. *Internal factors* are situations or determinants inside the company.

A. *Marketing objectives* are determined by the company's chosen target market and its position in the market overall. For example:
   1. Is the luxury market being sought?
   2. Is the economy market being sought?
   3. Is a survival strategy envisioned (selling below cost)?
   4. Will product prices be based on demand?
   5. Do research and development costs need to be covered?
B. The *marketing mix strategy* coordinates products along with production, distribution, and promotion to form a consistent and effective marketing program. Some examples include
   1. Target costing: Starting with the price the company wants to charge for a product then working backwards (changing production processes, simplifying systems, working with outside suppliers and distributors, deciding on a marketing campaign). Compaq did this years ago with their Prolinea personal computer line. First they determined what the production costs had to be in order to achieve the target price, then they changed their internal systems to meet the costs that would get them there.
   2. Value pricing: When the best strategy is not to charge the lowest price but to make the product different (or seem to be different) so that it's worth a higher price.
C. *Costs* are what the product actually costs to produce and market. **Fixed costs** are costs that do not vary with production, regardless of output (rent, heat, interest, depreciation, salaries, etc.). **Variable costs** vary according to output (labor, water, electricity, raw materials, etc.).
   1. **Cost-plus pricing** occurs when a standard markup is added after determining the fixed and variable costs of a product. This type of pricing is sometimes seen in construction companies or with lawyers, accountants, and other professionals who figure their costs then add 15 percent (or whatever).
II. *External factors* are situations or determinants outside the company.
   A. *The market and demand*:
      1. Pure competition: Basing prices on "the going price" (everybody else is doing it so we will as well).

2. Oligopolistic competition: Having few sellers that are highly sensitive to one another's pricing strategies (if one company changes its prices so will the others).
3. Monopoly pricing: The producer pricing as he or she sees fit.

B. *Consumer perceptions* or basing prices on what customers think constitutes value (*Note:* This requires a *firm* understanding of consumer behavior).

C. *Price-demand relationship* involves setting prices according to market demand.

D. *Competitor's costs, prices, and offers* include basing prices on the overall selling environment.

Pricing in Action

The following list provides explanations of the different types of pricing strategies, with examples of their application:

- *Breakdown:* Prices are broken down into palatable segments. A $1,000 gym membership is sold in installments (four payments of $250 or only $2.75 per day).
- *Seasonal:* Price is adjusted for certain periods of time. Prices rise during peak seasons or are reduced during slow times.
- *Pay one price* or *pay as you go:* This label is self-explanatory. In amusement parks, either pay one fee and ride all the rides, or pay for each ride separately.
- *Bundling* or *unbundling:* Services or products sold as a package deal or split up and sold separately, such as activities sold in lots such as ten aerobics classes or five tennis lessons. Unbundling would sell these as single units.
- *Exclusivity:* Paying for "snob appeal." Setting premium prices for trendiness or what is perceived as social esteem.
- *Discount:* Low prices. Customers buy because the price is low.
- *Captive:* "Locking in" customers by initially selling cheap then charging a premium for necessary components. A classic example are computer printers that are cheap, but the ink cartridges are very expensive.
- *Psychological:* Prices do not approach what is perceived as too much. For example, charging $99 instead of $100, or listing member prices next to nonmember's.

- *Promotional:* Not paying a set price. This strategy means having constant sales or always bettering what the competition charges.
- *Value added:* Adding "freebies" or other incentives without charging for them. Two-for-one deals or a baker's dozen are two examples.
- *Trials:* Easing the perceived risk by encouraging participation before closing the sale. Customers are offered the first tennis lesson free, or a ninety-day trial period, or perhaps money-back guarantees.
- *Hidden costs:* Not displaying extra costs needed to complete the product or service. This is done by not including tips, taxes, labor, parts, batteries, etc.
- *Fixed to variable:* One price begins the process, the next price(s) is determined by use. For example, pay to get into the disco, then for each drink.
- *Differential:* Charging customers differently. Members pay one price, nonmenbers pay another.
- *Creative variable:* Setting prices according to demand, but in an imaginative way. This means altering the price depending on certain variables (e.g., selling rope by the inch).
- *Price performance:* Price determined by value perception. For instance, museums or exhibits may ask guests to leave a donation instead of charging an entrance fee.
- *Differing segments:* Same product/service sold at different prices. Children, senior citizens, groups, adults, etc., each pay a different price.
- *Product line:* Prices arranged to get customers to focus on "the deal." Expensive goods may be displayed next to reasonably priced goods.

SUMMING UP PRICING

When setting prices, don't sell yourself short. Think about how high you can reasonably go rather than how low. Always consider what your customers will perceive as fair and ethical. Never stop analyzing why and how your business came up with its prices and don't be afraid to try new ways to achieve pricing satisfaction.

Chapter 30

Business Marketing and Promotion: A Checklist

This checklist was developed from a variety of sources—particularly the school of hard knocks. Most frontline business managers strive to do many of the things listed in the following section. However, everyone needs a little reminding from time to time of the attributes and nuances that make up the big picture. Whether you're a student or a manager, study the categories discussed in this chapter. With a little imagination, many of the suggestions mentioned can be used or altered so that they'll achieve the ultimate objective in every business—a sale. Just bear in mind that there is no middle ground here. The answer to each question must be 100 percent yes. Anything else means no.

IN-HOUSE MARKETING

Point-of-Sale Area

The **point-of-sale area** is where maximum customer flow occurs. To ensure a peaceful, informative, and professional selling environment, evaluate whether your company meets the following criteria:

yes/no   Adequate space to allow for efficient presentation of products on sale

yes/no   A setup and service that minimizes delays and queues

yes/no   Clean, well-lit display units allowing customers to examine products in a relaxed manner

yes/no   Careful product arrangement to avoid too many distractions during the point of sale yes/no   Walls cleared of clutter and signs because employees either don't want to confront customers or don't want to do their job (i.e., clean area after use, we do not take credit, etc.)

yes/no   Placing of essential products so that customers pass by when and where they are most likely to purchase them

yes/no   Pleasing colors and background music that keeps with the image of the business

In-Store Promotion

This involves advertising on the premises. Indicate which promotions your company employs:

yes/no   Special offers relating to specific product lines

yes/no   Personalities invited to attend functions who will attract customers to the premises (don't laugh, there are plenty of well-known people in their field who'll come and give a seminar and/or sign a book for the publicity and the price of a train ticket)

yes/no   Internal and external customer competitions offering attractive prizes or incentives (for example, the person bringing in the most paying customers wins)

yes/no   Merchandise with company logo (can also be used for prizes and giveaways, such as a free key chain or T-shirt with every sale)

yes/no   Provision of adequate promotional literature (leaflets, brochures, signs, coupons, etc.) (see section titled "Unique Selling Points")

In-Store Advertising

Evaluate whether your company fulfills the following requirements:

yes/no   Professional posters with the name of a product and its advertising message

yes/no   Staff uniforms neat, clean, and always worn

yes/no   Professional posters or displays to promote products, deals, promotions, or services yes/no   A well-informed staff that knows what it's doing and what's going on

yes/no   Well-stocked staff work areas (what message are you sending if a pen or other needed tool can't be found when and where it's needed?)

Internal Public Relations

Indicate which options your company has in place:

yes/no   Introduction of a suggestion box where customers are not afraid to deposit their remarks

yes/no   Introduction of a house journal, newsletter, or pamphlet

yes/no   Arrangement of social events for customers and their families

yes/no   Introducing incentives to reward employee productivity, customer loyalty, etc.

yes/no   Offering special discounts or services to employees (if your employees buy and use your products they'll probably encourage others to buy them too)

ycs/no   Providing effective training opportunities for employees (including letting employees attend seminars, lectures, and personal-growth workshops)

yes/no   Providing for employee participation in your business's decision making (particularly in setting up programs they envisioned or have a special interest in)

OUT-OF-HOUSE MARKETING

Unique Selling Points

Capitalize on what sets your business apart from others. Evaluate your company in terms of the following criteria:

yes/no   Trained staff (Can/does your staff help sell your business outside of work hours? Do you have a champion or award winner on board? Is he or she mentioned in your advertising?)

yes/no   Competitive prices

yes/no   Good location (with ample parking)

yes/no   Attractive peripheral service (late and early openings, delivery, installation, etc.)

yes/no   Introduction of special events ("open house" days, sales, parties or get-togethers, etc.)

yes/no   Provision of adequate promotional literature in the form of leaflets, brochures, signs, and coupons (It might be a good idea to have several different types, with each targeting a specific clientele. For example, one for walk-ins, one for corporate memberships, one for seniors or students, etc.)

yes/no   Use of testimonials from satisfied customers

Community Relations

Indicate whether your company participates in the following initiatives:

yes/no   Donations to local charitable causes (along with a story to the media stating this)

yes/no   Development of good relations with local media owners

yes/no   Introduction of your services to the local needy community (for example, a health club's facilities could be made available to a cardiac patient unit, physiotherapy businesses, a school or college, a community center, and so on)

yes/no   Introduction of special events or special days during which the community can be exposed to your business's operations

yes/no   Participation in local event sponsorship (and being allowed full advertising rights)

yes/no   Favorable contacts with local council members and chamber of commerce members

Direct Sales Campaigns

Evaluate your company's performance on the following sales techniques:

yes/no   Selling directly to the customer (direct mailings, personal visits, sales calls, etc.)

yes/no   Target marketing select individuals with advertising para-
phernalia (dropping off select-specific brochures at student
unions, companies or corporations, sport shops, waiting/
reception areas, the local tourist information center, etc.)

yes/no   Target marketing groups (personal visits to local clubs, ath-
letic teams, popular meeting places, company functions,
and so forth to let them know of special group prices)

yes/no   Having a booth at trade exhibits or fairs

yes/no   Press releases (one or two hundred words sent to the media
regarding information your business considers newswor-
thy)

yes/no   Invitations to the media (or other notables) to come look
over, try, and discuss your service

Indirect Sales Campaigns

Evaluate your company's use of these approaches:

yes/no   Sponsorship/advertising space at local sports venues or with
local team programs

yes/no   Media advertising (*Note:* With television, radio, and news-
papers, ascertain what demographic market they reach and
if they match your target market. The operators of these mediums *do* have this information.)

yes/no   Trade and technical journal advertising

yes/no   Advertising in special-interest magazines or coupon book-
lets that reach your target audience (e.g., tourist pamphlets,
student/university publications, etc.)

yes/no   Neon/lighted signs (located outside and/or hanging over the
sidewalk for all to see)

If you can't answer yes to the majority of these questions, you're
selling yourself short, and something needs to be done about it.

TIPS FOR MARKETING THAT OBTAINS RESULTS

• *Don't make your task too complicated* and *don't go it alone.* Use
your staff. The simpler the approach and the more people that
are involved the better.

- *Have fun.* What you create will reflect the atmosphere and environment from whence it came.
- *Don't fall in love with your own advertising.* The point of advertising is to attract customers, not to design something that appeals to you and your staff. All marketing efforts should marry the benefits being sought by paying customers with what is being offered. Do you know why your current customers came to your business to begin with?
- *Don't count on cleverness to attract customers.* The most effective marketing campaigns don't come from dazzling advertisements and eye-catching slogans. The marketing campaigns that bring in the most customers are usually the ones for which the marketing team did the most work.
- *Learn from the results.* If your marketing is a success, find out why. Don't simply let your staff pat each other on the back and walk away with the notion that they'll win again in the future.
- *If your marketing isn't a success, find out why.* Sometimes only one ingredient is missing. As the saying goes, those who fail often never realize how close to success they came. Avoid the old chestnut "We tried that once and it didn't work." If you've done your research, know your customers, and everyone gets involved and pulls in the same direction, it *will* work. You'll never know until everyone stops talking about it or fighting it and actually *does* it.

Chapter 31

Advice

About twelve years ago I was exercising in a gym on the Red Sea coast when a friend entered and hopped on the adjacent exercise bike. This guy made a *lot* of money working for a management consulting firm, and at some point I steered our conversation toward exactly what it was a management consultant did. My previous experiences with consultants resulted in the conclusion that they charged enormous sums of money for doing basic research and/or stating the obvious. "Tell me," I said, "when a company calls on you to do a consulting job, do you start a unique analysis from scratch? Or do you have a set of prewritten concepts that are reworked and presented as if they were tailor-made?"

He contemplated his answer for a long time. "The latter," he finally replied.

I laughed. "Do you think it's fair to say that most consulting jobs involve little more than erasing the name of the last client from the pages of a prewritten text and inserting the name of the next one?"

"Mostly, yes," he said.*

THE PIG DANCE:
DISCUSSION VERSUS ACTION

Too many companies are involved in what I call the PIG (**p**erpetual **i**nformation **g**athering) dance. All too often this dance is an illusion designed to fool everyone into thinking that continuous discussion,

---

*A friend who works in Africa recently e-mailed me with her opinion of consultants. "They use twenty-five words when one will do, they talk endlessly in circles, and they cringe whenever you ask them anything specific about practical application. Am I missing something?"

unending research, and infinite analysis is the raison d'être of management. Please understand that I'm not saying it's wrong to gather information in management; in fact gathering *pertinent* information is a basic necessity in every managerial position. What I'm talking about is the *dance*—the lining up at a company's trough to conduct endless analysis and partake in expensive trysts with consultants in order to produce reams of information that no one in the company bothers to do anything with. More often than not, the folks involved in the PIG dance are wallowing in procrastination at company expense, not to mention fobbing off their managerial duties onto someone else. For the most part, companies wishing to hire consultants should get off their backsides, get out of their offices, talk to their customers (not consultants), and do their own research. Remember, discussion, study, and analysis are a *part* of management—they're not supposed to be the end result. Equally as important, statistics should be seen as diagnostic tools, not operational blueprints. That being said, of course there are times when expertise may be needed in a specific area. For example, it would be foolish not to consult a lawyer when in need of legal advice or a safety expert for safety needs. Yet you should be *very* wary of those who give advice without ever having experienced its repercussions. The number of management consultants who have been fired from previous jobs because of incompetence, or were hired by a consulting firm fresh out of a university and can claim only "raking leaves" or "making french fries at a fast food restaurant" as experience, or who ran an amateurish (and now bankrupt) home business, is absolutely terrifying. Always do a thorough background check of a consultant, including contacting previous clients, before hiring one.

In most business environments, if you use the term *researcher* in place of *consultant* you're well on your way to understanding what it is that many people who call themselves consultants really do. The truth is that research isn't worth much if those who accumulate it can't, won't, or don't do anything with it. As the information technology director of a major United Kingdom bank once told me, "It's now an unwritten policy at my company to avoid hiring job candidates with PhDs." As he explained, his bank was fed up with people who could perform research but were clueless when it came to applying it (i.e., creating value).

Managing Is About Creating Value, Not Talking About It

Doing research and writing reports is easy. *Application* is what makes management difficult. The proof is in a story relayed to me by a seasoned practitioner. In fact, it's so well known I've even seen it dramatized on the BBC. Nevertheless, the obviousness of its message bears repeating.

One of the more notable consulting organizations in the world is McKinsey & Company. In fact, some estimates claim that almost two-thirds of the world's Fortune 1000 companies use McKinsey & Company when in need of a consultant. McKinsey & Company was founded in 1926, and took its name from its creator, James O. McKinsey. After several years of providing advice to some of the world's biggest corporations, Mr. McKinsey decided to crown his career by becoming the CEO of a major company. Such a move would not only solidify his reputation, he thought, but also the consulting business that bore his name. So in 1934, in the midst of the Depression, he accepted a position as chairman of the board of Marshall Field's, an acclaimed American retail institution. McKinsey began his chairmanship in earnest, quickly resorting to the cost-cutting measures and other astringent financial practices he'd been advising other companies to perform for years. Within two years after taking his post, however, it became apparent that these methods weren't working. Indeed, they seemed to have the opposite effect and Marshall Field's was soon brought to its knees. In desperation, the board of directors met behind McKinsey's back to determine how to get rid of him. McKinsey must have gotten wind of this meeting, for on the night it was conducted he collapsed and was rushed to hospital. He died a week later, but shortly before doing so he was overheard admitting to one of his assistants that in all the time he'd been a consultant *he'd never realized how difficult it was to be a manager* and *how wide the chasm was between management and consulting!*

IDEAS FOR IMPROVING YOUR BUSINESS

Along with just about everything else in this book, here are three more business improvement ideas that won't cost you the expense of a consultant. Bear in mind that these ideas aren't suitable for every business (*ideas* are found in books, not answers), but with a little creativity they can probably be reworked to suit one or two appropriate situations.

1. *Displaying productivity.* When I was in my twenties I heard about a factory foreman who regularly displayed what each of his employees had produced that day on a big board that everyone could see. The result was that everyone in the company knew who was pulling his or her weight and who wasn't. Ten years later I used a variation of this idea to keep track of sixty-two employees scattered across more than two dozen different work sites. The board was placed in the front office, and I displayed the names of those working off site, including where they were supposed to be, at what times, and several other bits of information. The result? Productivity tripled. An added benefit was that office workers could give customers detailed answers as to what was going on at these sites (something they'd had difficulty with before). It took a month to coax everyone into using the board, but once it became clear that it wasn't going away, it helped reduce my supervisory workload considerably. It also provided self-motivation and peer regulation for my employees.

2. *Multiple training.* There's a supermarket in my neighborhood that adheres religiously to this principle. Employees are rotated to different sections every week. The idea is to train each employee in several different jobs. That way, when someone is sick or quits, a temporary replacement can be found immediately from within. Rotating staff and having them perform many different tasks also has other benefits. It greatly reduces boredom, helps induce fresh new ideas, and tends to keep the pathways of communication open between employees.

3. *Saying yes.* Someone once asked me for the best piece of management advice I had. "Say *yes* more often than *no*," I replied. By prudently exploring all options and choosing the best one (saying yes), a manager explores new possibilities and constantly moves forward rather than standing still. Unfortunately, new and insecure managers are notorious for saying no. There are two reasons for this. The first is that they think saying no shows everyone who's boss (it doesn't). The second is that say-

ing yes translates into more work (as well as risk), which is true, but then again new ideas and practices always create more work initially. It's usually weeks or months afterward when the value of new ideas is most often seen—as well as the time and cost savings.

A BUSINESS NO-NO: LIVING IN THE SHORT TERM

Some companies (particularly large ones) seem to spend a lot of time and money concentrating on hype, spin, and media attention in order to appear successful. Unfortunately, these measures often do little more than strengthen a façade. Undoubtedly, glitz and showmanship do draw attention, but unless quality and service have increased in proportion to this hoopla, customers will wise up quickly. In other words, the major "paying-customer issues" (quality, service, value, speed, fairness, and convenience) that frontline managers and employees must contend with every day are the real building blocks of business. Just about everything else is window dressing. Businesses that build a strong foundation have a better chance of survival when economic or financial storms strike (which they inevitably do).

Living in the short term is seen in the leisure industry with bars or other venues that suddenly start charging an entrance fee for no apparent reason other than to get an extra five or ten dollars from paying customers. Of course, the ledger books look great the first week or so of this new policy, but after a while, if customers don't see any extra value connected with the new fee they'll take their patronage elsewhere. These business then have a very difficult time attracting both new and old customers once word spreads that they're just plain greedy.

Long-term business strategy revolves around earning money in exchange for a product or service and leaving customers with a desire to come back—not by making a lunge for the wallet of the first prospect who enters the door.

Chapter 32

An A-to-Z Business Success Primer

THE BASICS

AFFIRM YOUR PRIORITIES. Before succeeding in business, it's usually necessary to consider exactly what your company needs. The obvious answer is an increase in revenues, but how will this be done? Some options:

- Streamlining systems and/or operations
- Targeting a specific clientele
- Introducing a new product or service (or eliminating an old one)
- Improving customer service
- A combination of two or more of these (or other) objectives

If your organization is serious about succeeding then it's worth the time and effort to consider these questions, write them down, and then discuss them. By doing this, valuable input is gained from customers and a written guide can be formulated against which objectives can be measured.

BE PREPARED FOR RESISTANCE. Initiating changes not only means accepting that things will be done differently; it entails others accepting it too. Change is a difficult concept to preach. Few people like to abandon the comfort of the familiar and embrace the unknown. In most business situations, change is perceived as threatening because it involves accepting greater responsibilities.

Nonmanagerial employees' responsibilities include these:

- Accepting that the ownership of problems and solutions belongs to everyone in the business

- Understanding that work must equal value, and that it's not enough to show up and perform bottom-line duties
- Realizing that everyone must pull in the same direction (serve others)
- Caring about work by displaying integrity and trust

Managers must also face an expanded role and these responsibilities:

- Sharing information and providing complete and thorough training
- Viewing workers as assets
- Prudently choosing the right people for the right jobs
- Asking for, listening to, and then acting on other's viewpoints
- Rewarding good performance
- Ensuring that employees and departments endeavor to serve one another (pull in the same direction)

Make no mistake, the greatest difficulty in management often lies in providing employees with enough incentive to work hard. The good news is that management isn't rocket science. It doesn't take complex theories and formulas to succeed. Nor does it require a detailed set of blueprints. In fact, studies show that concrete plans and strict guidelines can be anathema to a business because they often result in a lack of flexibility and adaptability (and every organization *must* possess these qualities). So what does it take? To bolster the business arsenal and rediscover and awaken the human attributes that are found in every company, a need to work, the desire to excel, integrity, perseverance, loyalty, and fairness must exist. These are every company's greatest assets because they provide the impetus behind *every* success. Just as important, they cost nothing.

CUSTOMERS MUST BE THE FOCUS OF ALL WORK. All changes should lead to this concept. Keep in mind that the definition of a customer is *everyone that an organization serves.* In its broadest sense, this includes everyone encountered at work, not just people who exchange money for goods and services. In order for true customer care to be achieved, managers must get out of their ivory towers and walk along the front lines (the areas where customers are served). The idea is not to look over shoulders but to *listen,* learn, and formulate improvements and solutions from a whole new angle.

- Are all products, services, and systems designed based on what customers want and *how* they want them? (Don't think a business can dictate terms to paying customers.)
- Is the business concentrating so hard on one market that other potential markets are being excluded? (Customers have the ability to pick and choose. Businesses do not.)
- Do all attitudes thrive by the creed that it's everyone's job to serve both internal and external customers? (No one is too busy to help.)

It can't be made clearer—if customers don't like what they see or hear, they'll take their business elsewhere. Employees who know of their importance to the organization and who fully appreciate their responsibilities within it have the ability to provide good service. Customer care emanates best from people who feel they are genuinely part of a team.

DELEGATE. Encourage and train employees to handle problem-solving. Teach them to recognize and solve the *cause* of problems, not just the *effect*. Bear in mind that a common mistake made by many businesses is to-the-bone cost-cutting that squeezes the life out of the organization. Yes, regularly cutting expenses is paramount to every business, but doing so by reducing quality or laying off workers is not a viable long-term solution. *Revenues don't come from cost-cutting. Revenues come from customers—and customers must be sought and earned.* In other words, use your frontline employees to get closer to your paying customers and win them over. The buzz-word here is *empowerment* (i.e., motivating employees for their own reasons, not the business's reasons).

- Provide employees with enough information and leeway to make decisions and formulate ideas.
- Work to harness the energy created by the inevitable conflicts that will arise.
- Join together to modify ideas so that (1) they will fit customer's needs and (2) the people who must work with these concepts *will* work with them.
- Delegate, don't abdicate, when employees think of, and apply, their own solutions.

The point is that a business should rely on itself for solutions because of its unique relationship with its customers. Be wary of consultants and the exorbitant fees that come with them. Don't eliminate boldness and risk and learn to handle conflict functionally (not dysfunctionally). Remember, there's a lesson in every objection and mistake. At the very least, failure or disagreement means that somebody had the courage to take action. If employees aren't performing to expectations, the fault usually lies with management for (1) not selecting the right person for the job, (2) providing insufficient information and training, or (3) not creating an atmosphere conducive to achievement.

ETHICS AND QUALITY ARE ESSENTIAL ELEMENTS IN ALL PHASES OF BUSINESS SUCCESS. It may be a cliché, but what goes around does come around. Never underestimate the intelligence of internal or external customers by shortchanging them. With so much choice available to customers these days, quality and ethics can't be overstated. When conducting business, be honest, say what you mean, mean what you say, and provide the very best. Reputations are priceless and, like customers, a good reputation must be earned. To enable ethical decision making, try these approaches:

- Understand the real reasons or intentions behind your company's decisions.
- Be aware of the outcome of every action or behavior.
- Show accountability with decision making.
- Comprehend the whole picture.

A good rule of thumb is to always think in the long term. Short-term solutions, by sheer design, are destined to cause trouble in the future. And the future is coming.

FORGE AHEAD. The missing catalyst in leading a successful business is often *action*—a decisive leap into uncharted waters. Don't let analysis lead to paralysis. Stick your neck out and get on with it!

- Divide goals into manageable, comprehensive steps.
- Communicate details clearly and often.
- Provide all the continuous training needed.
- Be patient and allow commitment to grow.

GALLANTRY. A good way to manage others successfully is to set a good example. I once managed a business that included several very large and busy facilities. Naturally, every hour produced some type of mess that had to be cleaned up, and I used to constantly needle the staff to make doing this a habit. Several employees came from countries in which this was considered demeaning, so one day, after asking them for the umpteenth time to clean up something and not getting any response, I did it myself. Within minutes the entire staff was helping. They never had to be asked again. The message? Authority works best when it radiates rather than is wielded.

H Sorry. But from here on out, you and your employees are on your own. Welcome to management.

AN ANALOGY

It might sound strange, but managing a business is comparable to entering an equestrian show-jumping competition. If you don't know much about show jumping, you're in good company. Most people who become managers have no idea what they're getting into either. Just as in business and management, in a show-jumping competition both horse and rider are attempting an untried situation for the first time. Nobody knows the outcome because steering a horse that might have other ideas over a series of formidable obstacles during the heat of competition is very different from boastfully envisioning the end result. The best advice on offer is to tackle each jump as it comes— one at a time.

Among the numerous obstacles that turn up on a course, there's usually one comprised of four or five (or more) hurdles set in a tight row. These are called bounce jumps. The difficulty with bounce jumps lies in the horse's ability to bound quickly over them. The solution is to aim for the center of the last jump and spur the horse on.

If you're serious about improving your business, your aim as a manager (that last hurdle) is to work toward becoming redundant— a difficult thing for insecure people to understand. In effect, it means setting up your business (or department) so that, as much as possible, it runs itself. The result is a workforce that prevents problems as well as responds to them, thereby avoiding the emotional and financial drain of being in a perpetual state of crises.

A popular adage states that several people, each wanting to pursue a separate destination, can be put on the back of a horse, but a horse can only go in one direction. Are you ready? Okay. Gather up your reins. The buzzer has sounded and your name's been called. It's time to exit the warm-up ring and enter the course. Keep in mind that in management there is no finish line—if you're in it, you're in it for the long haul. Yes, it's scary, but many times in life you must act even though you are afraid. And right now, the only obstacle standing between you and victory is that first leap.

Giddyup.

Glossary

accommodation: Letting someone else have his or her way in order to end a conflict.

actual product: What a business sells (and that which separates one product from another) in terms of parts, quality, features, design, and packaging that combine to deliver core product benefits.

adaptive organization: An organizational design that has little bureaucracy, reacts well to change and the environment, has few layers of management, and encourages the input of employees.

adjourning: The process of concluding a meeting or gathering.

administration: The people who set policies in a business and/or comprise the executive level of that business, or the management team of a public or nonprofit organization.

advertising: Any paid form of presentation and promotion of a product that does not involve personal selling.

attribution theory: A theory that helps explain the ways in which people interpret the behavior of others by, in part, suggesting that human actions are either internally or externally caused.

augmented product: The additional services and benefits incorporated with a core product (such as installation, after-sale service, sales, warranties, delivery, credit, and so forth).

autonomy: Independence or self-rule. In management, autonomy refers to the ability to act without constantly seeking approval or permission from superiors.

behavior modification: Changing people's behavior with rewards or punishment.

benchmarking: Comparing a product or business with another product or business to gain ideas that will result in an improvement.

benefit perception: The advantage, value, or profitable gain paying customers seek when buying a product or service.

brainstorming: The stimulation and free flow of opinions and ideas among people in a nonthreatening environment.

breadth: In business, a term that refers to the expansive layout of a company's hierarchical structure (i.e., all the departments) from top to bottom and left to right. *See also* DEPTH

bureaucracy: Usually seen today as an organization built on formality, a rigid chain-of-command authority, and many layers of management. Characteristically, bureaucracies tend to have many rules and regulations, reams of paperwork, and respond poorly to change.

bureaucratic organization: *See* BUREAUCRACY and MECHANISTIC ORGANIZATION

celebrity CEO: A chief executive officer who spends inordinate amounts of time and effort garnering attention.

chain of command: The uninterrupted direction a command or request takes through an organization, or a line of authority that links someone in an organization with someone else in that same organization.

change: To alter, vary, or modify something in some way.

communication: The sending, receiving, and understanding of meaning.

competitive advantage: An edge or trait that enables a business to do better than its competitors.

conflict: Disagreement, either seen or unseen, over an issue or issues of substance.

consultant: A person who is paid to give information, advice, or an opinion. In business, more often than not, a consultant is someone who produces research.

controlling: An act of responsibility and power that involves monitoring results and, if needed, taking action.

core culture: The aspects of an organization's culture that are not readily seen (how employees are judged, levels of worker involvement, quality of work life, etc.).

core product: The benefit consumers seek when they purchase a product.

corrective communication: Feedback designed to correct a behavior.

cost-plus pricing: Adding a standard markup to a product or service after determining fixed and variable costs.

culture: A learned set of beliefs, values, and patterns of behaviors common to groups or nations.

culture shock: The confusion, discomfort, and disorientation experienced by individuals after moving to another country or culture.

customer database: Information that explains a paying customer's details including address, economic description, buying habits, income level, possible future needs, and so on.

customers: Everyone whom an organization serves.

decentralization: Awarding managers the authority (autonomy) to make decisions without having to constantly consult a head office.

decision making: Identifying a problem then analyzing and choosing from corrective solutions.

delegation: Entrusting the completion of a task to one or more people by giving them the authority to think and act for themselves.

department: The separate divisions within an organization, or a group of people in an organization working as a unit and sharing a common duty or specialization under one manager.

depth: A term commonly associated with change management that refers to all the people in every department within a business. The term also implies that these people are aware of and fully involved in the functioning of the business. *See also* BREADTH

dysfunctional conflict: Always seeing conflict as a black-or-white issue or a battle that must be won. *See also* FUNCTIONAL CONFLICT

empowerment: The act of giving ongoing authority to an employee (or employees) by giving them the autonomy to think and act for themselves.

escalating commitment: Continuing to pour money, time, and effort into something that is not working.

ethics: Standards that determine what is acceptable or unacceptable in regard to behavior (i.e., what is good or bad or right or wrong).

evaluation: The formal judgment of an employee's performance.

external customers: The people who buy products or services who are not affiliated with or employed by the business.

feedback: The opinion, advice or correction given to someone who is performing, about to perform, or has just completed a task.

filtering: Altering information before passing it along to a superior or colleague to make it appear more favorable.

fixed costs: The costs of producing a product or service that do not change when production output volumes increase or decrease (rent, salaries, interest, heating and air conditioning, etc.).

forecast: An attempt to predict the future based on legitimate data.

formatting: To arrange in a particular order or way.

forming: Selecting people who will be assigned to work as a team.

functional conflict: Calmly encouraging, respecting, and listening to opposing views in order to reduce mistakes, clear the air, and come up with or improve ideas and solutions.

fundamental attribution error: Assuming that a person's behavior is the result of internal rather than external causes, or being wrong when trying to determine the cause of something.

goal: A specific result that an individual or organization expects to achieve.

group think: When a group's desire to reach agreement takes precedence over everything else and results in poor performance.

guidelines: Loose descriptions that dictate behavior and/or state what is or isn't expected.

heuristics: A process or strategy that oversimplifies decision making.

hierarchical pyramid: A triangle-shaped diagram showing either the chain of command of an organization or that ranks the importance or order of something.

humanism: The study of human personality and behavior in regard to motivation and the fulfillment of an individual's potential.

internal customers: The people who work within an organization (employees) and those who are a part of it (suppliers, contractors, shareholders, and other stakeholders) who need and rely on one another.

leadership: The influence of one person over another (or others) to strive toward the fulfillment of a goal or goals.

leading: Acquiring followers, maintaining morale, and motivating others while pursuing a common goal.

learning: The process of acquiring information that leads to permanent change.

management: Please refer to Chapter 1.

marketing: The act of bringing a buyer and seller together for the purpose of a sale or commitment.

mechanistic organization: Another term for bureaucracy (i.e., an organization built on formality, a rigid chain-of-command authority, many layers of management, many rules and regulations, reams of paperwork, and a poor response to change).

meeting: A gathering of people designed to convey information, brainstorm, and formulate possible answers or concrete solutions to customer-related problems.

mission statement: A broad outline briefly describing an organization as well as stating what it does, what it thinks is important, and where it's headed.

networking: Building and maintaining positive interrelationships with people.

norming: When a team settles down and begins to work.

norms: Informal rules adopted by a group to control behavior.

objectives: The specific results that a person or organization hopes to achieve (similar to goals).

observable culture: What one sees and hears when walking around a business that makes the business unique and instills it with a sense of character and unity.

organic organization: An organizational design that has little bureaucracy, reacts well to the environment, has few layers of management, and greatly encourages the input of employees.

organization: A group of people with formally designed roles who work together to achieve a common, agreed-upon purpose.

organizational culture: A learned set of traits and characteristics that establishes an organization's tone and practices and guides the behavior of its people.

organizational structure: The way an organization and its offices (chain-of-command authority and communication links) are arranged.

organizing: Clarifying, dividing, and arranging activities or work in order to produce a goal or goals.

performing: When a team agrees on a system that allows it to get to work and culminate individual efforts into a single shared outcome.

personal selling: The use of face-to-face oral presentation with one or more perspective customers for the purpose of making a sale and building a relationship.

plan: An idea and its implementation devised to accomplish a goal.

planning: Setting goals, courses of action, procedures, and the allocation of resources while forecasting future results.

point-of-sale area: The area in a business where money is exchanged for products or services.

presentation: A formal or informal display of information given by a person or a team of people that is designed to convey information and achieve a set goal.

proactive change: Preparing for change before it occurs.

problem solving: Identifying a discrepancy between an actual situation and a desired result and then taking action to rectify any problems.

product: The goods or services an organization manufactures, produces, and/or sells.

product life cycle: The course of a product's sales from development to its introduction and on to its growth, maturity, and decline.

project: A planned set of actions leading to a single (often marketable) result.

public relations: The building of relations with the public by obtaining favorable publicity and creating a good image.

quality: A degree of excellence that meets or exceeds customer expectations.

reactive change: Trying to deal with change after it occurs.

recession: A period of economic decline, usually identified when the gross national product falls for two successive quarters, characterized by sluggish product demand, the failure of real output to rise, and unemployment increases.

role: The position a person takes in an organization including what he or she is expected to perform.

rules: Strict and specific descriptions that dictate behavior and/or state what is or isn't expected.

sales promotion: Short-term incentives designed to encourage the purchase of a product.

selective perception: Looking at situations or problems from a limited point of view.

sensory adaptation: Becoming so accustomed to something that it's often taken for granted.

service: Assistance, aid, value, or cooperation given to others.

skill: An above-average ability to convert knowledge into action.

social loafing: The tendency of some individuals to reduce their input or effort when working in a group.

span of control: The number of people who report directly to a manager.

storming: The personality clashes, bids for domination, faction forming, and fights that typically arise shortly after a group of people has been assigned to work together.

strategy: Preparing for the future by doing everything possible to strengthen yourself and your organization in the here and now.

stress: A state of debilitating tension suffered when trying to cope with demands, situations, or constraints.

subculture: Small, independent cultures that exist within the larger culture of an organization.

synergy: When the end result of something is greater than the sum of its parts.

team: A group of people committed to a common purpose for which they work and hold themselves mutually accountable.

termination: A permanent and forced act that severs a person from an organization (usually due to incompetence, incompatibility, or illegal or unethical behavior).

value: The merit, caliber, or usefulness a person sees in something or someone else.

values: The underlying beliefs of what people feel is unimportant or important as well as what they should or should not do.

variable costs: The costs inherent in producing goods or services that vary according to production output (wages based on time, raw materials, electricity, etc.).

vision: In a business sense, vision refers to a simple and highly motivating means to unite people toward a common purpose and direction while invoking their emotions (lifting their hearts and minds).

visual aids: Items used to highlight or dramatize an issue or point in a presentation.

whistle-blowing: The practice of exposing the unethical or illegal behavior of others.

work: Effort partaken outside of personal time and usually done in exchange for money, favor, or validation, or activity that produces value for others.

work group: A group of people who share information, work together, and help one another to meet common goals and produce results (to a manager, a *work group* is more or less the same as a *team*).

Bibliography

Chapter 1

Collins Cobuild English Language Dictionary, William Collins and Co Ltd., London/Glasgow, 1988.

Kotter, J.P., "What Effective General Managers Really Do," *Harvard Business Review,* vol. 60, November-December 1974, pp. 156-157.

Longman Dictionary of Contemporary English, Longman Group UK Ltd., Harlow, 1988.

Merriam-Webster's Collegiate Dictionary (11th Edition), Merriam-Webster Inc., Springfield, MA, 2003.

The New Oxford English Dictionary, Oxford University Press, Oxford, 1993.

Schermerhorn, J.R., *Management* (Fifth Edition), John Wiley & Sons, New York, 1996.

Smith, A. *An Inquiry into the Nature and Causes of Wealth of Nations* (Fourth Edition). Edwin Cannon (Ed.), Methuen Publishing Ltd., London, 1925.

Chapter 2

Duncan, W.J., *Great Ideas in Management,* Jossey-Bass, San Francisco, 1989.

Fayol, H., *Industrial and General Administration,* Dunod, Paris, 1916.

Jones, S.R.G., "Was There a Hawthorne Effect?" *American Journal of Sociology,* November 1992, pp. 451-468.

Kanigel, R., *The One Best Way,* Viking Press, New York, 1997.

Linden, D.W., "The Mother of Them All," *Forbes Magazine,* January 16, 1995, pp. 75-76.

Roethlisberger, F.J. and Dickson, W.J., *Management and the Worker,* Harvard University Press, Cambridge, MA, 1939.

Weber, M., *The Theory of Social and Economic Organization,* Free Press, New York, 1947.

Chapter 3

"Back to Basics," Survey: Management, *The Economist,* March 9, 2002, pp. 3-18.

Boyatzis, R.E., *The Competent Manager,* John Wiley & Sons, New York, 1982.

Outcome Measurement Project of the Accreditation Research Committee, American Assembly of Collegiate Schools of Business, 1984.

Sorenson, R., "A Lifetime of Learning to Manage Effectively," *The Wall Street Journal,* February 28, 1983, p. 18.

Chapter 4

Kanter, R.M., "Transcending Business Boundaries," *Harvard Business Review,* May-June 1991, pp. 151-154.

Leonard, S., "Love That Customer," *Management Review,* October 1987, pp. 36-39.

Lorinc, J., "Now the Customer is Job 1," *Canadian Business,* July 1997, pp. 22-28.

"A Matter of Priorities," *The New York Times,* February 19, 1995, section F, p. 23.

Oakland, J., *Total Quality Management,* Butterworth-Heinemann, New York, 1993.

Scott, J.T., *Fundamentals of Leisure Business Success: A Manager's Guide to Achieving Success in the Leisure and Recreation Industry,* The Haworth Press, Binghamton, NY, 1998.

Chapter 5

Fishman, C., "The Wal-Mart You Don't Know," Fast Company, issue 77, December 2003, p. 68. Available at www.fastcompany.com/magazine/77/walmart.html.

Handy, C., *Understanding the Organization,* Penguin Books Ltd., London, 1993.

Katz, R.L., "Skills of an Effective Administrator," *Harvard Business Review,* September-October 1974, pp. 90-102.

Lau, A.W. and Pavett, C.M., "Managerial Work: The Influence of Hierarchical Level and Functional Specialty," *Academy of Management Journal,* March 1983, pp. 170-177.

Matteson, M.T., "Some Reported Thoughts on Significant Management Literature," *Academy of Management,* June 1974, pp. 386-389.

McGregor, D., *The Human Side of Management,* McGraw-Hill, New York, 1960.

Pascale, R.T., *Managing on the Edge,* Penguin Books, New York, 1991.

Wren, D.A., *The Evolution of Management Thought,* John Wiley & Sons, New York, 1994.

Chapter 6

Carnegie, D., *How to Win Friends and Influence People,* Simon & Schuster, New York, 1939.

Caudron, S., "Delegate for Results," *Industry Week,* February 6, 1995, pp. 27-28.

Lewicki, R.J., Bowen, D.D., Hall, D.T., and Hall, F.S., *Experiences in Management and Organizational Behavior* (Third Edition), John Wiley & Sons, New York, 1988.

Robbins, S.P. and Hunsaker, P.L., *Training in Interpersonal Skills* (Second Edition), Prentice-Hall, Saddle River, NJ, 1996.

Scott, J.T., *Fundamentals of Leisure Business Success: A Manager's Guide to Achieving Success in the Leisure and Recreation Industry,* The Haworth Press, Binghamton, NY, 1998.

Semler, R., *Maverick: The Success Story Behind the World's Most Unusual Workplace,* Warner Books, New York, 1995.

Whetton, D.A. and Cameron, K.S., *Developing Management Skills* (Third Edition), HarperCollins, New York, 1991.

Chapter 7

Burns, T. and Stalker, G.M., *The Management of Innovation,* Oxford University Press, Oxford, 1994.

Chandler, A.D., "Origins of the Organizational Chart," *Harvard Business Review,* March-April 1988, pp. 156-157.

Deal, T. and Kennedy, A., *Corporate Cultures,* Penguin Books, New York, 1988.

Harrison, R. "How to Describe Your Organization," *Harvard Business Review,* September-October 1972.

Hesselbein, F., Goldsmith, M., and Beckhard, R., *The Leader of the Future,* Jossey-Bass, San Francisco, 1996.

Hesselbein, F., Goldsmith, M., and Beckhard, R., *The Organization of the Future,* Jossey-Bass, San Francisco, 1997.

Schein, E.H., "Organizational Culture," *American Psychologist,* vol. 45, 1990, p. 109.

Sellers, P., "So you Fail . . . Now Bounce Back," *Fortune,* May 1, 1995, p. 49.

Chapter 8

Band, W., *Creating Value for Customers,* John Wiley & Sons, New York, 1991.

Chatwin, B., *Anatomy of Restlessness,* Picador, London, 1996.

Cole, G., *Management: Theory and Practice,* DP Publications, London, 1991.

Lewin, K., *Field Theory in Social Science,* Harper Press, New York, 1951.

Schein, E.H., *Process Consultation: Its Role in Organizational Development,* Addison-Wesley Press, 1969.

Strebel, P., "Choosing the Right Change Path," *The Financial Times* (part 14), February 9, 1996, p. 5.

Chapter 9

Filley, A.C., *Interpersonal Conflict Resolution,* Scott Foresman, Glenview, IL, 1975.

Kreitner, R., "Personal Wellness: It's Just Good Business," *Business Horizons,* vol. 25, May-June 1982, pp. 28-35.

Pascale, R.T., *Managing on the Edge,* Penguin Books, New York, 1991.

Peters, T.J. and Waterman, R.H., *In Search of Excellence: Lessons from America's Best-Run Companies,* Harper & Row, New York, 1983.

Robbins, S.P., "Conflict Management and Conflict Resolution Are Not Synonymous Terms," *California Management Review,* Winter 1978, p. 71.

Thomas, K.W. and Schmidt, W.H., "A Survey of Management Interests with Respect to Conflict," *Academy of Management Journal,* June 1976, pp. 315-318.

Walton, R.E., *Interpersonal Peacemaking: Confrontations and Third-Party Consultation,* Addison-Wesley, Reading, MA, 1969.

Chapter 10

Clegg, C.W., "Outcomes of Autonomous Workgroups," *Academy of Management Journal,* June 1986, pp. 280-284.

Cohen, S.G., Ledford, G.E., and Spreitzer, G.M., "A Predictive Model of Self-Managing Work Teams," *Human Relations,* May 1996, p. 644.

Robbins, H. and Finley, M., *Why Teams Don't Work,* Pacesetter Books, Princeton, NJ, 1995.

Tuckman, B.W., "Developmental Sequence in Small Groups," *Psychological Bulletin,* vol. 63, 1965, pp. 384-389.

Waterman, R.H., Peters, J., and Phillips, J.R., "Structure Is Not Organization," *Business Horizons,* vol. 23, no. 3, June 1980, pp. 14-26.

Chapter 11

Bart, C.K., "Sex, Lies, and Mission Statements," *Business Horizons,* November-December 1997, p. 11.

Kerr, S., "Overcoming the Dysfunctions of MBO," *Management by Objectives,* vol. 5, no. 1, 1976.

McConkey, D.D., *How to Manage by Results,* AMACOM, New York, 1976.

Robbins, S.P. and Hunsaker, P.L., *Training in Interpersonal Skills* (Second Edition), Prentice-Hall, Upper Saddle River, NJ, 1996.

Chapter 12

"Benchmarkers Make Strange Bedfellows," *Industry Week,* November 15, 1993, p. 8.

Deming, W.E., *Out of the Crisis,* The W. Edwards Deming Institute & The MIT Center for Advanced Engineering, Cambridge, MA, 1986.

Garvin, D.A., "Competing on the Eight Dimensions of Quality," *Harvard Business Review,* vol. 65, no. 6, 1987, pp. 101-109.

Lawler, E.E. and Mohrman, S.A., "Quality Circles After the Fad," *Harvard Business Review,* January-February 1985, pp. 65-71.

Main, J., "How to Steal the Best Ideas Around," *Fortune,* October 19, 1992, pp. 102-106.

Sashkin, M. and Kiser, K.J., *Putting Total Quality Management to Work,* Berret-Koehlor, San Francisco, 1993.

Chapter 13

Gellerman, S.W., "Why Good Managers Make Bad Ethical Choices," *Harvard Business Review,* vol. 64, July-August 1986, pp. 85-90.

Government Accountability Project as reported in "Blowing the Whistle Without Paying the Piper," *Business Week,* June 3, 1991, pp. 138-140.

Nash, L.L., "Ethics Without the Sermon," *Harvard Business Review,* November-December 1981, p. 81.

Otten, A.L., "Ethics on the Job," *The Wall Street Journal,* July 14, 1986, p. 17.

Chapter 14

Blake, R.R., Mouton, J.S., Barnes, L.B., and Greiner, L.E., "Breakthrough in Organization Development," *Harvard Business Review,* November-December 1964, p. 136.

Drucker, P.F., "Leadership: More Doing than Dash," *The Wall Street Journal,* January 6, 1988, p. 16.

Fiedler, F.E., "Time Based Measures of Leadership Experience and Organizational Performance," *Leadership Quarterly,* Spring 1992, p. 5.

Hersey, P. and Blanchard, K.H., *Management of Organizational Behavior,* Prentice-Hall, Englewood Cliffs, NJ, 1988.

House, R. (Goal Path Theory), see: Huber, G.P., "A Theory of Effects of Advanced Information Technologies on Organizational Design, Intelligence, and Decision Making," *Academy of Management Review,* vol. 15, 1990, p. 67.

"The Jack and Jeff Show Loses its Luster," *The Economist,* May 4, 2002, pp. 63-65.

Kirkpatrick, S.A. and Locke, E.A., "Leadership: Do Traits Matter?" *Academy of Management Executive,* vol. 5, May 1991, pp. 48-60.

Nielsen, J. and Vollers, M., *Icebound: A Doctor's Incredible Battle for Survival at the South Pole,* Hyperion, NY, 2001.

Vroom, V.H. and Jago, A.G., *The New Leadership,* Prentice-Hall, Englewood Cliffs, NJ, 1988.

Chapter 15

McGregor, D., *The Human Side of Enterprise,* McGraw-Hill, New York, 1960.

Wren, D.A., *The Evolution of Management Thought* (Fourth Edition), John Wiley & Sons, New York, 1994.

Chapter 16

Cox, T., "The Multi-Cultural Organization," *Academy of Management Executive,* vol. 5, May 1991, p. 34.

Emmons, S., "Emotions at Face Value," *The Los Angeles Times,* January 9, 1998, p. E1.

Gullahorn, J.T. and Gullahorn, J.E., "An Extension of the U-Curve Hypothesis," *Journal of Social Sciences,* January 1963, pp. 34-47.

Hofstede, G., "Cultural Constraints in Management Theories," *The Executive,* February 1993, pp. 81-99.

Mole, J., *Mind Your Manners: Culture Clash in the European Single Market,* Industrial Society Press, London, 1990.

Munter, M., "Cross-Cultural Communication for Managers," *Business Horizons,* May-June 1993, pp. 69-77.

Penrose, J.M., *Business Communication: Strategies and Skills,* Dryden Press, Chicago, 1988.

Rafaeli, A. and Sutton, R.I., "The Expressions of Emotion in Organizational Life" used in Cummings, L.L. and Staw, B.M., *Research in Organizational Behavior,* JAI Press, Greenwich, CT, vol. 11, 1989, p. 8.

Robbins, S.P. and Hunsaker, P.L., *Training in Interpersonal Skills* (Second Edition), Prentice-Hall, Upper Saddle River, NJ, 1996.

Schermerhorn, J.R., *Management and Organizational Behavior,* John Wiley & Sons, New York, 1996.

Scott, J.T., *Fundamentals of Leisure Business Success: A Manager's Guide to Achieving Success in the Leisure and Recreation Industry,* The Haworth Press, Binghamton, NY, 1998.

Chapter 17

Agor, W.H., *Intuition in Organizations,* Sage Publishing, Newbury Park, CA, 1989.

Hogarth, R.H., Kahneman, D., and Tversky, A., *Judgements in Managerial Decision Making* (Third Edition), John Wiley & Sons, New York, 1994.

Huber, G.P., *Managerial Decision Making,* Scott Foresman, Glenview, IL, 1975.

Pounds, W., "The Process of Problem Finding," *Industrial Management Review,* Fall 1969, pp. 1-19.

Simon, H.A., *Administrative Behavior,* Free Press, New York, 1947.

Von Oech, R., *A Kick in the Seat of the Pants,* Harper & Row, New York, 1986.

Chapter 18

Blair, G.M., *Starting to Manage: The Essentials Skills,* The Institute of Electrical & Electronics Engineers, Piscataway, NJ, 1996.

Drucker, P.F., *The Effective Executive,* Harper & Row, New York, 1967.

Griessman, B.E., *Time Tactics of Very Successful People,* McGraw-Hill, New York, 1996.

McCay, J.T., *The Management of Time,* Prentice-Hall, Englewood Cliffs, NJ, 1995.

Webber, R.A., *To Be a Manager,* Irwin Press, Homewood, IL, 1981.

Chapter 19

Alderfer, C.P., *Existence, Relatedness, and Growth,* Free Press, New York, 1992.

Herzberg, F., "One More Time: How Do You Motivate Employees?" *Harvard Business Review,* vol. 47, January-February 1968, pp. 54-63.

Luthens, F. and Kreitner, R., *Organizational Behavior Modification,* Scott Foresman, Glenview, IL, 1975.

Maslow, A.H., *Motivation and Personality* (Second Edition), Harper & Row, New York, 1970.

Matteson, M.T., "Some Reported Thoughts on Significant Management Literature," *Academy of Management Journal,* June 1974, pp. 386-389.

McClelland, D.C., *The Achieving Society,* Van Nostrand, New York, 1961.

Meyer, H.H., "A Solution to the Performance Appraisal Feedback Enigma," *The Executive,* February 1991, pp. 68-76.

Chapter 20

Berlo, D.K., *The Process of Communication,* Holt-Rinehart & Winston, New York, 1960.

Carnegie, D., *How to Win Friends and Influence People,* Simon & Schuster, New York, 1939.

Hall, E.T., *The Silent Language,* Doubleday, New York, 1973.

Kursh, C.O., "The Benefits of Poor Communication," *The Psychoanalytic Review,* Summer-Fall, 1971, pp. 189-208.

Peters, T. and Austin, N., *A Passion for Excellence,* Random House, New York, 1985.

Tannen, D., "The Power of Talk: Who Gets Heard and Why," *Harvard Business Review,* September-October 1995, pp. 138-148.

Chapter 21

Armstrong, M., *How to Be an Even Better Manager,* Kogan Page, London, 1990.
Filipczak, B., "Obfuscation Resounding: Corporate Communication in America," *Training,* July 1995, p. 36.
Gwynne, S.C. and Dickerson, J.F., "Lost in the E-Mail," *Time Magazine,* April 21, 1997, pp. 88-90.
Lengel, R.H. and Daft, R.L., "The Selection of Communication Media as an Executive Skill," *Academy of Management Executive,* vol. 2, Aug 1988, p. 225.
Semler, R., *Maverick,* Warner Books, New York, 1995.

Chapter 22

Blair, G.M., *Starting to Manage: The Essentials Skills,* The Institute of Electrical & Electronics Engineers, Piscataway, NJ, 1996.
Lahiff, J.M. and Penrose, J.M, *Business Communication: Strategies and Skills,* Dryden Press, Chicago, 1988.
Lengel, R.H. and Daft, R.L., "The Selection of Communication Media As an Executive Skill," *Academy of Management Executive,* vol. 2, August 1988, pp. 225-232.
Robbins, S.P. and Hunsaker, P.L., *Training in Interpersonal Skills: Tips for Managing People at Work* (Second Edition), Prentice-Hall, Upper Saddle River, NJ, 1996.

Chapter 23

Armstrong, M., *How to Be an Even Better Manager,* Kogan Page, London, 1990.
Hingston, P., *The Greatest Little Business Book,* Hingston, London, 1979.

Chapter 24

Blair, G.M., *Starting to Manage: The Essentials Skills,* The Institute of Electrical & Electronics Engineers, Piscataway, NJ, 1996.
Scott, J.T., *Fundamentals of Leisure Business Success: A Manager's Guide to Achieving Success in the Leisure and Recreation Industry,* The Haworth Press, Binghamton, NY, 1998.

Chapter 25

Kotler, P., Armstrong, G., Saunders, J., and Wong, V., *Principles of Marketing* (Second European Edition), Prentice-Hall Europe, London, 1999.

Murphy, P.E. and Enis, B.M., "Classifying Products Strategically," *Journal of Marketing,* July 1986, pp. 24-32.

Chapter 26

Coyne, K.P., "Sustainable Competitive Advantage: What It Is, What It Isn't," *Business Horizons,* vol. 29, no. 1, January-February 1986, pp. 54-61.

Porter, M.E., *Competitive Advantage,* Free Press, New York, 1985.

Porter, M.E., *Competitive Strategy: Techniques for Analyzing Industries and Competitors,* Free Press, New York, 1980.

Thompson, A.A. and Strickland, A.J., *Strategic Management* (Seventh Edition), Richard Irwin, Inc., Boston, 1993.

Chapter 27

Bennet, P.D., *Dictionary of Marketing Terms,* American Marketing Association, Chicago, 1988.

Farber, B. and Wycoff, J., "Customer Service: Evolution and Revolution," *Sales and Marketing Management,* May 1991, pp. 47-53.

Kotler, P., Armstrong, G., Saunders, J., and Wong, V., *Principles of Marketing* (Second European Edition), Prentice-Hall Europe, London, 1999.

Scott, J.T., *Fundamentals of Leisure Business Success: A Manager's Guide to Achieving Success in the Leisure and Recreation Industry,* The Haworth Press, Binghamton, NY, 1998.

Chapter 28

Scott, J.T., *Fundamentals of Leisure Business Success: A Manager's Guide to Achieving Success in the Leisure and Recreation Industry,* The Haworth Press, Binghamton, NY, 1998.

Chapter 29

Cateora, P.R., *International Marketing* (Seventh Edition), Irwin Press, Homewood, IL, 1990.

Nagle, T.T. and Holden, R.K., *The Strategy and Tactics of Pricing* (Second Edition), Prentice-Hall, Englewood Cliffs, NJ, 1995.

Schwartz, D.J., *Marketing Today: A Basic Approach* (Third Edition), Harcourt Brace Jovanovich, New York, 1981.

Scott, J.T., *Fundamentals of Leisure Business Success: A Manager's Guide to Achieving Success in the Leisure and Recreation Industry,* The Haworth Press, Binghamton, NY, 1998.

Chapter 30

Halloran, J.W., *The Entrepreneur's Guides to Starting a Successful Business* (Second Edition), McGraw-Hill, New York, 1992.

Schwartz, D.J., *Marketing Today: A Basic Approach* (Third Edition), Harcourt Brace Jovanovich, New York, 1981.

Scott, J.T., "Effective Marketing," *Recreation Magazine,* March/April 1996, pp. 5-6.

Scott, J.T., "Good Customer Care," *Hospitality,* August-September 1996, p. 15.

Tomkinson, L., "Tips for Improving Retail Sales," *Update,* July-August 1997, pp. 5-8.

Chapter 32

Scott, J.T., "Raising the Dead," *Entrepreneur,* February 2001, pp. 67-69.

Index

Page numbers followed by the letter "f" indicate figures.

Order a copy of this book with this form or online at:
http://www.haworthpress.com/store/product.asp?sku=5399

THE CONCISE HANDBOOK OF MANAGEMENT
A Practitioner's Approach

_____in hardbound at $49.95 (ISBN-13: 978-0-7890-2647-7; ISBN-10: 0-7890-2647-3)

_____in softbound at $29.95 (ISBN-13: 978-0-7890-2648-4; ISBN-10: 0-7890-2648-1)

Or order online and use special offer code HEC25 in the shopping cart.

<table>
<tr><td>COST OF BOOKS_____</td><td>☐ BILL ME LATER: (Bill-me option is good on US/Canada/Mexico orders only; not good to jobbers, wholesalers, or subscription agencies.)</td></tr>
<tr><td>POSTAGE & HANDLING_____
(US: $4.00 for first book & $1.50 for each additional book)
(Outside US: $5.00 for first book & $2.00 for each additional book)</td><td>☐ Check here if billing address is different from shipping address and attach purchase order and billing address information.

Signature_____</td></tr>
<tr><td>SUBTOTAL_____</td><td>☐ PAYMENT ENCLOSED: $_____</td></tr>
<tr><td>IN CANADA: ADD 7% GST_____</td><td>☐ PLEASE CHARGE TO MY CREDIT CARD.</td></tr>
<tr><td>STATE TAX_____
(NJ, NY, OH, MN, CA, IL, IN, PA, & SD residents, add appropriate local sales tax)</td><td>☐ Visa ☐ MasterCard ☐ AmEx ☐ Discover
☐ Diner's Club ☐ Eurocard ☐ JCB
Account # _____</td></tr>
<tr><td>FINAL TOTAL_____
(If paying in Canadian funds, convert using the current exchange rate, UNESCO coupons welcome)</td><td>Exp. Date_____

Signature_____</td></tr>
</table>

Prices in US dollars and subject to change without notice.

NAME_____

INSTITUTION_____

ADDRESS_____

CITY_____

STATE/ZIP_____

COUNTRY_____ COUNTY (NY residents only)_____

TEL_____ FAX_____

E-MAIL_____

May we use your e-mail address for confirmations and other types of information? ☐ Yes ☐ No
We appreciate receiving your e-mail address and fax number. Haworth would like to e-mail or fax special discount offers to you, as a preferred customer. **We will never share, rent, or exchange your e-mail address or fax number.** We regard such actions as an invasion of your privacy.

Order From Your Local Bookstore or Directly From
The Haworth Press, Inc.
10 Alice Street, Binghamton, New York 13904-1580 • USA
TELEPHONE: 1-800-HAWORTH (1-800-429-6784) / Outside US/Canada: (607) 722-5857
FAX: 1-800-895-0582 / Outside US/Canada: (607) 771-0012
E-mail to: orders@haworthpress.com

For orders outside US and Canada, you may wish to order through your local
sales representative, distributor, or bookseller.
For information, see http://haworthpress.com/distributors

(Discounts are available for individual orders in US and Canada only, not booksellers/distributors.)

PLEASE PHOTOCOPY THIS FORM FOR YOUR PERSONAL USE.
http://www.HaworthPress.com   BOF04